Manual of Operational Techniques for Self-Mounted Patrols

Officer JeanMark S.

Copyright © 2024 Officer JeanMark S.

All rights reserved.

ISBN: 9798320042299

DEDICATION

This book is dedicated to the brave men and women who serve as police officers every day. You stand on the front lines, protecting our communities and upholding the law. You face danger with courage, navigate complex situations with reason, and strive to build trust and understanding. Your dedication to public safety and your commitment to justice deserve our deepest respect and gratitude. May this book serve as a resource to support you in your endeavors, guide you through challenges, and inspire you to continue your vital service.

Thank you for all that you do.

TABLE OF CONTENTS

INTRODUCTION 11

PART 1 - FOUNDATIONAL SKILLS FOR SAFE PATROLLING 13

    MAINTAINING OFFICER SAFETY 14

        Situational awareness and threat assessment: your shield on the street 14

        De-escalation techniques and verbal judo: turning down the heat 16

        Officer wellness and self-care: fueling your resilience 19

    COMMUNICATION AND INTERPERSONAL SKILLS .. 22

        Effective communication with the public: bridging the gap 22

        Active listening and conflict resolution: diffusing tension with understanding 23

        Cultural competency and de-bias training: building Bridges, not walls 25

        Building rapport and trust with the community: the foundation for safety 27

    VEHICLE OPERATIONS AND PATROL TECHNIQUES 29

        Safe driving practices for patrol vehicles: your patrol car isn't a race car 29

        Effective search patterns for buildings and areas: leaving no stone unturned 31

        Utilizing technology for communication and information gathering: your digital partner 33

        Recognizing and reporting suspicious activity: your eyes and ears on the street 34

PART 2: OPERATIONAL PROCEDURES FOR COMMON SCENARIOS 36
TRAFFIC STOPS AND VEHICLE SEARCHES 37
Initiating traffic stops with minimal risk: a measured approach 37
Approaching and interacting with motorists: professionalism and courtesy 39
Documenting traffic violations and issuing citations: thorough records for accurate enforcement 41
Conducting lawful vehicle searches based on probable cause 43
INVESTIGATING SUSPICIOUS PERSONS 46
Identifying indicators of suspicious behaviour: reading between the lines 46
Approaching and questioning individuals: De-escalation and information gathering 48
Field identification procedures (FIPs) and stop-and-frisk tactics: balancing officer safety with individual rights 50
Recognizing potential mental health situations: when intuition meets training 52
ARRESTS AND USE OF FORCE 55
Apprehension techniques and handcuffing procedures: taking control safely 55
De-escalation strategies during arrests: prioritizing a peaceful resolution 57
Legal justification and documentation of the use of force: transparency and accountability 60
Reporting and after-action review of arrest procedures: learning from every encounter 62
CRIME SCENE MANAGEMENT 65
Securing and isolating the crime scene: preserving a pristine picture 65
Initial investigation and evidence preservation: building the foundation for a case 67

Interviewing witnesses and gathering information: unveiling the pieces of the puzzle 70
Cooperation with detectives and crime scene technicians: building a cohesive investigative team 72
DOMESTIC VIOLENCE INTERVENTION 76
Recognizing signs of domestic violence: intervening before escalation 76
De-escalation tactics and victim safety protocols: prioritizing calm and protection 78
Reporting and victim support resources: empowering healing and accountability 83

PART 3: PSYCHOLOGICAL ASPECTS AND TEAMWORK 85
COPING WITH STRESS AND TRAUMA 86
Understanding the impact of police work on mental health 86
Techniques for stress management and emotional resilience: building inner strength 88
Critical incident stress debriefing (CISD) resources: processing trauma as a team 91
Maintaining a healthy work-life balance: fueling your well-being 93
THE IMPORTANCE OF PARTNERSHIP 96
Effective communication and collaboration with patrol partner: building a cohesive unit 96
Recognizing signs of stress and supporting your partner: a pillar of partnership 98
Building trust and mutual respect within the partnership: the foundation of success 101
Utilizing each other's strengths for optimal results: a team advantage 103
LEGAL CONSIDERATIONS AND REPORT WRITING 106
Understanding relevant laws and department policies: a foundation for effective action 106

Techniques for stress management and emotional resilience: building inner strength 108
Critical incident stress debriefing (CISD) resources: processing trauma as a team 111
Maintaining a healthy work-life balance: fueling your well-being 113
THE IMPORTANCE OF PARTNERSHIP **116**
Effective communication and collaboration with patrol partner: building a cohesive unit 116
Recognizing signs of stress and supporting your partner: a pillar of partnership 118
Building trust and mutual respect within the partnership: the foundation of success 121
Utilizing each other's strengths for optimal results: a team advantage 123
LEGAL CONSIDERATIONS AND REPORT WRITING 126
Understanding relevant laws and department policies: a foundation for effective action 126
Accurate and comprehensive report writing: the power of documentation 128
Documenting events and actions in a clear and concise manner: capturing the essence of the encounter.. 130
Courtroom testimony and evidence presentation: delivering a compelling account 133
CONTINUING EDUCATION AND PROFESSIONAL DEVELOPMENT **136**
Importance of ongoing training and skill development: a commitment to excellence 136
Staying up-to-date on new laws, procedures, and technologies: navigating a dynamic landscape 138
Seeking mentorship and peer support opportunities: building a network for growth 141
Maintaining professional integrity and ethical conduct: the cornerstone of trust 143

CONCLUSIONS **146**
ABOUT THE AUTHOR **152**

DISCLAIMER

The information contained in this book is for informational purposes only and does not constitute professional advice or training. While every effort has been made to ensure the accuracy and completeness of the information presented, the publisher and author disclaim any liability or responsibility for errors or omissions.

This book should not be used as a substitute for official departmental training or established police procedures. Officers should always refer to their department's policies and guidelines for the most up-to-date information and protocols.

The use of specific tactics, procedures, or technologies described in this book may not be suitable for all situations and should be adapted based on departmental regulations, individual circumstances, and applicable laws.

Readers are encouraged to seek professional guidance from qualified instructors and legal counsel when necessary.

INTRODUCTION

The streets can be quite dynamic and full of surprises. As a police officer, on patrol you play a role in upholding public safety and maintaining order. This guide is designed to provide you with the knowledge and skills to handle the situations you may encounter during your daily rounds.

This detailed manual goes beyond the basics delving into skills that ensure your safety, such as awareness and de escalation techniques. You will learn ways to communicate with the community establish trust and leverage technology for outcomes.

It's essential to master procedures. The manual covers everything from traffic stops and vehicle searches to interacting with suspects and following arrest protocols, all while adhering to guidelines and best practices. You'll also gain expertise in managing crime scenes intervening in violence situations and navigating scenarios.

Police work involves more than following protocols; it also acknowledges the emotional challenges of the job. You'll receive guidance on stress management tools, building resilience against trauma, and maintaining a work-life balance. Establishing a partnership with your patrol partner is crucial for success. The manual offers insights on fostering communication, trust and mutual respect to create a team that excels in any situation.

Lastly, this manual underscores the importance of learning throughout your career.

Understanding the significance of learning, keeping up with changes, and seizing chances for career growth are crucial aspects.

As you progress in your profession always uphold behavior. This guidebook serves as your ally equipping you with the expertise and abilities required to serve your community with professionalism, security and empathy. Lets commence your adventure as a self initiated police officer.

PART 1 - FOUNDATIONAL SKILLS FOR SAFE PATROLLING

MAINTAINING OFFICER SAFETY

Situational awareness and threat assessment: your shield on the street

Before we delve into the details, let's set the stage. Situational awareness and threat assessment are crucial skills for law enforcement officers, security personnel, and anyone interested in improving their safety. Now, imagine a scene: you're responding to a noise complaint as you approach the address, a group of people gathers on the porch, their body language tense. One individual stands out, hand resting near their pocket.

This is where situational awareness comes in. You're actively collecting information – the number of people, their positioning, nonverbal cues – to paint a mental picture of the unfolding situation.

Situational awareness is your constant companion. It's about being hyper-vigilant to your surroundings, anticipating potential threats, and constantly evaluating the scene. Here's how to hone this critical skill:

- Pay attention to detail: Don't let routine blind you. Notice suspicious behaviour, environmental hazards, and potential escape routes.

- Scan the environment systematically: Don't let your gaze wander. Develop a systematic approach to taking in the scene, ensuring you miss nothing.

- Be mindful of non-verbal cues: Body language, facial expressions, and tone of voice can speak volumes. Learn to interpret these cues to assess potential threats.

- Maintain a heightened state of alertness: Complacency is your enemy. Stay focused, even in seemingly calm situations.

Threat assessment builds on situational awareness.

By analyzing the information you gather, you can estimate the likelihood of violence or danger. Consider these factors:

- The individual's behaviour: Are they agitated, aggressive, or reaching for concealed objects?

- The presence of weapons: Are there visible weapons or objects that could be used as weapons?

- Criminal history or known risk factors: Is there any information about the individuals involved that suggests a heightened risk?

MANUAL OF OPERATIONAL TECNIQUES FOR SELF-MOUNTED PATROLS

By constantly assessing the situation, you can adapt your approach. Sometimes, a calm demeanour and clear communication can de-escalate a tense situation. In other cases, you may need to call for backup or take immediate action to protect yourself and others. Remember, your safety is paramount. By developing a keen sense of situational awareness and threat assessment, you'll be well-equipped to navigate the complexities of the street and make informed decisions to keep yourself safe.

De-escalation techniques and verbal judo: turning down the heat

Not every situation requires force. De-escalation techniques are your first defence in calming tense situations and preventing violence. Here's where verbal judo comes into play. Dr. George Thompson developed verbal judo as a communication approach that uses active listening, empathy, and assertive language to gain control of a conversation and steer it towards a peaceful resolution.

Imagine this: a motorist pulled over for speeding becomes argumentative and belligerent. De-escalation tactics can help defuse the situation. Here's how:

- Active listening: Closely to the person's words and body

language. Acknowledge their concerns and frustrations.

- Empathy: Show that you understand their perspective, even if you disagree. Phrases like "I can see why you're upset" can go a long way.

- Use "I" statements: Own your actions and requests. Instead of "You need to calm down," try "I understand you're frustrated, but let's try to work this out calmly."

- Offer choices: Empower the individual by providing options. "Would you like to step out of the vehicle, or would you prefer me to wait here?"

Verbal judo techniques build on these principles:

- Broken record: Repeat your request calmly and firmly, ignoring insults or provocations.

- Minimizing: Acknowledge a person's anger but downplay its severity. "I understand you're frustrated, but it's a minor issue."

- Fogging: Agree with a small aspect of their argument without conceding the whole point. "Yes, I understand you've had a long day, but..."

De-escalation isn't about giving in; it's about gaining control of the situation. Using verbal judo techniques and maintaining a calm demeanour, you can often de-escalate a situation and avoid unnecessary force. Remember, de-escalation is a skill that takes practice. The more you use these techniques, the more comfortable and practical you'll become.

Use of force continuum and legal considerations: a measured response

Force should always be a last resort. The use of force continuum is a framework that guides officers in responding to threats with a level of force proportional to the situation's severity. It's a spectrum, ranging from officer presence to deadly force.

Imagine this: a suspect resists arrest but doesn't pose a weaponized threat. The use of force continuum helps dictate the appropriate response. Here's the breakdown:

- Officer Presence: Your presence can often deter crime or de-escalate a situation. Use clear communication and a confident demeanour to assert your authority.

- Verbal Commands: Clear, concise instructions are essential. Direct the individual to comply with your requests and explain the consequences of non-compliance.

- Physical Control: Non-violent techniques like handcuffing or restraining holds may be necessary to control a resisting individual.

- Less-lethal Force: Pepper spray, tasers, or other non-lethal tools can be used to subdue a suspect who poses a threat but doesn't warrant deadly force.

- Deadly Force: This is the most extreme option and should only be used as a last resort to protect yourself or others from imminent serious bodily harm or death.

Legal considerations are paramount when using force. The critical principle is reasonableness. The severity of the threat, the actions of the suspect, and the potential for harm to yourself or others all factor into whether your use of force was justified.

Remember, using force continuum is a guide, not a rigid script. Every situation is unique, and your response should be based on the specific circumstances you encounter. Documenting your actions and decisions thoroughly is crucial for legal purposes and after-action review. Understanding the use of force continuum and its legal implications ensures that your actions are measured, appropriate, and defensible.

Officer wellness and self-care: fueling your resilience

The demands of police work can take a toll. Witnessing traumatic events, long hours, and the constant potential for danger can lead to stress, burnout, and even mental health issues.

Officer wellness and self-care aren't luxuries; they're essential for maintaining physical and mental well-being and, ultimately, effectiveness as officers.

Prioritize your physical health:

- Maintain a healthy diet: Fuel your body with nutritious foods to give yourself the energy you need to perform at your best.

- Get Sleep enough: Chronic sleep deprivation can impair judgment and reaction time. Aim for 7-8 hours of quality sleep each night.

- Exercise regularly: Physical activity is a powerful stress reliever and mood booster. Find an exercise routine you enjoy and stick to it.

Don't neglect your mental health:

- Develop healthy coping mechanisms: Find healthy ways to manage stress, such as meditation, yoga, or spending time in nature.

- Build a robust support system: Talk to friends, family, or a therapist about your challenges.

- Seek help when needed: Don't be afraid to seek professional help for stress, anxiety, or other mental health concerns.

Maintaining a healthy work-life balance is crucial.

Schedule time for hobbies, spend time with loved ones and disconnect from work when possible. This could mean turning off your work phone, avoiding checking work emails at home, or setting clear boundaries between work and personal life. Remember, taking care of yourself isn't selfish; it allows you to be a better officer, a better partner, and a better friend. By prioritizing your well-being, you'll be better equipped to handle the challenges of the job and serve your community with resilience and strength.

COMMUNICATION AND INTERPERSONAL SKILLS

Effective communication with the public: bridging the gap

As a self-mounted patrol officer, your interactions with the public are constant and varied. Effective communication is the cornerstone of building trust and rapport with the community you serve. Here are some key strategies to ensure clear and productive communication:

- Be clear, concise, and professional: Everyone can understand plain language. Avoid jargon and technical terms.

- Actively listen: Closely to the person's words and body language. Show them you're engaged and interested in what they have to say.

- Be respectful and empathetic: Treat everyone with dignity, regardless of their background or situation. Acknowledge their feelings and concerns.

- Use verbal de-escalation techniques: Maintain a calm and professional demeanour, even in tense situations. Avoid inflammatory language or accusatory tones.

- Practice active listening: Ask clarifying questions, paraphrase to ensure understanding, and acknowledge their perspective.

Effective communication is a two-way street. By actively listening and tailoring your communication style to your audience, you can bridge the gap between the police and the public. This fosters trust, cooperation, and a sense of shared responsibility for community safety. Remember, transparent and professional communication is a powerful tool for de-escalating situations, gathering information, and building positive relationships with the people you serve.

Active listening and conflict resolution: diffusing tension with understanding

The ability to listen actively is a superpower for any officer. It's the foundation for conflict resolution, transforming tense situations into opportunities for understanding and cooperation. Here's how active listening empowers you to de-escalate conflict:

- Focus on understanding, not judgment: Set aside your assumptions and truly listen to the person's perspective. Pay close attention to both verbal and nonverbal cues.

- Acknowledge their emotions: Validate their feelings, even if you disagree with their actions. Phrases like "I understand you're frustrated" can go a long way.

- Ask open-ended questions: Encourage the person to elaborate on their concerns. This helps you gather information and identify the root cause of the conflict.

- Summarize and paraphrase: Restate what you've heard to ensure understanding. This demonstrates that you're paying attention and builds trust.

By practising active listening, you create a safe space for open communication. This allows you to:

- Identify common ground: Look for areas where you agree, even if minor. This can be a springboard for finding a solution that works for everyone.

- Offer options and solutions: Work collaboratively to find a resolution that addresses their concerns and aligns with the law.

- De-escalate tension: Active listening helps calm emotions and fosters a more cooperative atmosphere.

Active listening is an investment in positive outcomes. By truly understanding the other person's perspective, you can navigate conflict with empathy and find solutions that benefit everyone involved. Remember, fostering cooperation through active listening builds trust within the community and makes your job safer and more effective.

Cultural competency and de-bias training: building Bridges, not walls

Policing a diverse community requires a deep understanding of different cultures and backgrounds. Cultural competency equips you to interact effectively with people from all walks of life. This, coupled with de-bias training, helps you recognize and challenge unconscious biases that might influence your judgment.

Imagine responding to a noise complaint in a neighbourhood with a significant immigrant population. Cultural competency allows you to understand the potential for miscommunication due to language barriers or cultural norms. Here's why it matters:

- Building trust and rapport: When you demonstrate an understanding of different cultures, you build trust and rapport with the community you serve. This fosters cooperation and information sharing.

• De-escalating conflict: Cultural competency allows you to recognize situations where cultural misunderstandings might be fueling conflict. You can then adjust your communication style to de-escalate the situation.

• Fair and impartial policing: De-bias training helps you identify and challenge unconscious biases that might influence your interactions with the public. This ensures fair and impartial treatment for everyone.

Cultural competency and de-bias training aren't one-time events; they're ongoing processes. Here are some ways to stay engaged:

• Seek out training opportunities: Participate in workshops and seminars focused on cultural competency and implicit bias.

• Build relationships within the community: Engage with diverse community groups to gain a deeper understanding of their values and perspectives.

• Reflect on your interactions: Regularly assess your own biases and consider how your actions might be perceived by people from different backgrounds.

By actively developing cultural competency and embracing de-bias training, you become a more effective and trusted officer. You'll build stronger relationships within the community, fostering a safer and more inclusive environment for everyone.

Building rapport and trust with the community: the foundation for safety

The key to effective policing isn't just about enforcement; it's about building trust and rapport with the community you serve.

This positive relationship is the foundation for a safer and more collaborative environment. Here's how to cultivate trust:

• Be approachable and professional: Maintain a friendly and respectful demeanour. Project an aura of helpfulness and a genuine desire to serve the community.

• Engage in positive interactions: Don't wait for calls for service to be your only contact with the public. Strike up conversations with residents, attend community events, and participate in outreach programs.

- Show empathy and understanding: Acknowledge community concerns and frustrations. Please demonstrate that you understand the challenges they face.

- Listen to their needs: Actively listen to residents' concerns and suggestions. This two-way communication fosters a sense of partnership and collaboration.

- Be transparent and accountable: Explain your actions and decisions clearly. Be open to feedback and willing to address community concerns.

Building trust takes time and consistent effort. When you demonstrate a genuine interest in the community's well-being, you create a positive feedback loop.

Residents become more willing to report crime, cooperate with investigations, and act as your eyes and ears on the street. This collaborative approach ultimately leads to a safer and more secure environment for everyone. Remember, building trust and rapport isn't a one-time act; it's an ongoing process that requires continuous effort and dedication. By consistently demonstrating professionalism, empathy, and a commitment to community service, you'll be well on your way to fostering a strong and trusting relationship with the people you serve.

VEHICLE OPERATIONS AND PATROL TECHNIQUES

Safe driving practices for patrol vehicles: your patrol car isn't a race car

Your patrol vehicle is your mobile office, but it's also a powerful machine. Safe driving practices are paramount for your safety, the safety of others, and the successful completion of your duties. Here are some fundamental principles to remember:

- Maintain focus and avoid distractions: Minimize distractions like using your phone or radio unless absolutely necessary. Keep your eyes on the road and anticipate potential hazards.

- Drive defensively: Assume other drivers might make mistakes. Maintain a safe following distance, avoid tailgating, and be aware of your blind spots.

- Obey traffic laws: Set a positive example by following the same rules of the road you enforce. Speeding, reckless driving, or ignoring traffic signals undermines public trust.

- Adjust your driving to weather conditions: Slow down during rain, snow, fog, or high winds. Increase your following distance and be extra cautious on slick roads.

- Utilize emergency lights and sirens safely: Only activate emergency equipment when responding to a call for service or pursuing a suspect. Use them judiciously to avoid startling other drivers and causing accidents.

- Practice emergency manoeuvres: Regularly participate in training exercises to hone your skills in emergency braking, swerving, and other manoeuvres you might encounter during high-speed chases or evasive actions.

Remember, a patrol car is a valuable tool, but it's only as safe as the person behind the wheel. By prioritizing safe driving practices, you'll minimize the risk of accidents, protect yourself and others, and ensure you arrive at your destination ready to serve your community effectively.

Effective search patterns for buildings and areas: leaving no stone unturned

During your patrols, you might encounter situations requiring a systematic search of a building or a large outdoor area. Employing effective search patterns ensures thorough coverage and minimizes the chance of missing crucial evidence or suspects. Here are some common search patterns and their strengths:

• Grid Search: This method is ideal for large, open areas with good visibility. Officers divide the area into smaller grids and systematically search each section, ensuring no spot is overlooked.

• Zone Search: Best suited for buildings or smaller enclosed spaces, the zone search assigns specific zones to each officer. This allows for a more detailed examination of each area while maintaining officer safety through teamwork.

• Strip Search: This linear search pattern works well for extended, narrow areas like roadways or fields. Officers proceed in a line, shoulder-to-shoulder, carefully examining both sides as they move forward.

• Spiral Search: Used in situations where a specific point of origin is known, like a reported gunshot location. Officers start at that central point and move outwards in a widening spiral pattern, expanding the search area methodically.

Choosing the correct search pattern depends on several factors, including:

• Size and layout of the area: Open fields call for tactics different from those used in complex buildings.

• Visibility: Limited visibility might necessitate a more detailed search pattern.

• Number of officers available: The available manpower will influence the chosen pattern's scope and intensity.

• Urgency of the situation: A time-sensitive search might require a faster, less detailed pattern initially, with a more thorough follow-up search later.

Effective communication is crucial during any search.

Officers should clearly define boundaries, maintain visual or auditory contact, and report any findings promptly. Remember, a well-executed search pattern is a powerful tool for ensuring officer safety, gathering evidence, and, ultimately, resolving the situation effectively.

Utilizing technology for communication and information gathering: your digital partner

Technology has become an indispensable partner in modern policing. Learning to utilize technology effectively for communication and information gathering enhances your safety, efficiency, and overall effectiveness. Here are some key ways technology empowers you:

• Mobile Data Terminals (MDTs): These in-car computers provide real-time access to critical information. You can access license plate registrations, criminal history databases, and outstanding warrants, allowing for swifter verification and informed decision-making.

• Automated Vehicle Location (AVL): AVL systems track patrol car locations, enabling dispatchers to efficiently assign resources and ensure your safety. Knowing your location allows for faster backup arrival in critical situations.

• Body-Worn Cameras (BWCs): BWCs provide a vital record of interactions with the public. They offer transparency and accountability, protecting both officers and citizens. Recordings can also serve as valuable evidence in court.

• Digital Communication Systems: Secure digital radios and messaging systems ensure precise and reliable communication with dispatch and other officers. This allows for seamless coordination and rapid response to unfolding situations.

- Databases and Information Sharing: Modern law enforcement databases offer a wealth of information, from criminal records to stolen vehicle reports. Effective utilization of these resources can lead to quicker identification of suspects and faster resolution of cases.

Remember, technology is a tool, not a replacement for critical thinking and sound judgment. Always prioritize officer safety and legal protocols when using any technological resource. By mastering these tools, you'll enhance your situational awareness, improve communication, and ultimately, better serve your community.

Recognizing and reporting suspicious activity: your eyes and ears on the street

A critical aspect of self-mounted patrol is being vigilant and recognizing suspicious activity. You are the first line of defence, and your ability to identify potential threats can deter crime and keep your community safe. Here are some key things to look for:

- Individuals: People acting nervous, out of place, or loitering around closed businesses at unusual hours might warrant further investigation. Please pay attention to erratic behaviour, attempts to conceal themselves, or excessive focus on your patrol car.

- Vehicles: Vehicles with obscured license plates, driving erratically, or parked in unusual locations can be a cause for concern. Look for signs of tampering, open trunks in deserted areas, or multiple occupants switching positions frequently.

- Locations: Open doors or windows in unoccupied buildings, signs of forced entry, or unusual activity around financial institutions like banks or ATMs might indicate criminal activity. Trust your gut instinct – if something seems off, it probably is.

Effective reporting is crucial. When you observe suspicious activity, document it thoroughly.

Here's what to include:

- Specific details: Provide a detailed description of the individuals, vehicles, or locations involved. Note clothing descriptions, license plate numbers, and any distinguishing features.

PART 2: OPERATIONAL PROCEDURES FOR COMMON SCENARIOS

TRAFFIC STOPS AND VEHICLE SEARCHES

Initiating traffic stops with minimal risk: a measured approach

Traffic stops are a common occurrence for self-mounted patrol officers. However, they can also be inherently risky situations. By prioritizing officer safety and utilizing a measured approach, you can minimize risk and ensure a safe and controlled stop. Here's how to initiate a traffic stop with minimal risk:

• Initial Observation: Before activating your lights, carefully observe the vehicle and driver's behaviour. Look for signs of impairment, erratic driving, or potential hazards within the vehicle.

• Safe Location: Choose a well-lit, open area with a wide shoulder for the stop. Avoid busy intersections or narrow roads with limited visibility. This allows for safe manoeuvring and reduces the risk of accidents.

- Request Backup: Whenever possible, especially during nighttime stops or if the violation appears serious, request backup from another officer before initiating the stop. Having additional support ensures your safety and allows for a more controlled interaction.

- Clear Communication: Once you've chosen a safe location, activate your emergency lights and siren, signalling the driver to pull over. Use clear and concise hand signals to guide them to the curb.

Officer positioning is critical:

- Approach with caution: Maintain a safe distance from the vehicle as you approach. Never stand directly in front of the driver's window. Aim to make contact at the passenger-side window, increasing the barrier between you and the driver.

- Body language: Project a calm and confident demeanour. Avoid aggressive posturing or making sudden movements that could be misinterpreted as a threat.

By following these steps, you can initiate a traffic stop with a focus on safety for yourself and the motorist. Remember, a measured approach that prioritizes clear communication and officer safety sets the stage for a successful and controlled interaction.

Approaching and interacting with motorists: professionalism and courtesy

After initiating a traffic stop, your next steps involve approaching and interacting with the motorist. Professionalism and courtesy are key throughout this interaction. Here's how to maintain a safe and controlled environment:

• Body language: Maintain a calm and professional demeanour. Avoid aggressive posturing or sudden movements that could startle the driver.

• Verbal communication: Greet the driver respectfully and explain the reason for the stop. Use clear and concise language, avoiding jargon or technical terms.

• Requesting identification: Politely ask the driver for their license, registration, and proof of insurance. Maintain a safe distance while they retrieve the documents.

Observe the driver and occupants closely:

• Signs of impairment: Look for bloodshot eyes, slurred speech, or the odour of alcohol or drugs. These signs may warrant further investigation for potential DUI (Driving Under the Influence).

- Nervousness: Excessive fidgeting, sweating, or difficulty maintaining eye contact could indicate the driver is concealing something. Be mindful, but avoid jumping to conclusions.

- Number of occupants: Be aware of the number of people in the vehicle and their positioning. This awareness helps you plan your approach and maintain control of the situation.

Here are some additional tips for a smooth interaction:

- Listen actively: Pay attention to the driver's explanation and respond calmly.

- Avoid arguments: If the driver becomes argumentative, remain calm and professional. Focus on de-escalation and obtaining the necessary information.

- Be transparent: Explain your next steps, whether it's issuing a citation, conducting a vehicle search, or releasing them with a warning.

By prioritizing professionalism, clear communication, and keen observation, you can effectively interact with motorists during a traffic stop.

Remember, courtesy and a calm demeanour go a long way in de-escalating potential tension and ensuring a safe and productive interaction.

Documenting traffic violations and issuing citations: thorough records for accurate enforcement

Traffic enforcement is a core function of self-mounted patrol. Thorough and accurate documentation is vital for ensuring a fair and legally sound process, from observing the violation to issuing a citation. Here's how to effectively document and address traffic violations:

• Gather all necessary information: Record the date, time, and location of the stop. Note the specific violation observed, along with the vehicle's make, model, and license plate number. Document the driver's license information and any passengers present.

• Witness statements: If there were any witnesses to the violation, obtain their statements and contact information. Witness accounts can be crucial evidence in court proceedings.

• Detailed narrative: Write a clear and concise narrative describing the events leading to the stop, the observed violation, and the driver's demeanour. Include details like weather conditions, lighting, and any observations about the vehicle's condition.

Issuing citations requires accuracy and clarity:

- Citation selection: Select the appropriate citation for the specific violation observed. Ensure all relevant information is accurately entered, including the driver's information, vehicle details, and the nature of the offence.

- Explaining the citation: Clearly explain the violation to the driver and answer any questions they might have. Inform them of their options, such as paying the fine, contesting the citation in court, or requesting a driving improvement course.

- Professional courtesy: Maintain a professional and courteous demeanour throughout the interaction. Treat the driver with respect, even if they are contesting the citation.

Detailed and accurate documentation serves several purposes:

- Court proceedings: Clear records provide essential evidence if the citation is contested in court.

- Departmental review: Documentation allows for supervisory review and ensures officers are adhering to proper procedures.

- Statistical analysis: Traffic stop data helps identify areas with high accident rates or frequent violations, allowing for targeted enforcement strategies.

By prioritizing thorough documentation and clear communication when issuing citations, you contribute to a fair and efficient legal system and ensure accurate data collection to guide future enforcement efforts.

Conducting lawful vehicle searches based on probable cause

The Fourth Amendment protects citizens from unreasonable searches and seizures. However, during a traffic stop, officers can conduct a vehicle search under specific circumstances. The fundamental justification for a lawful search is probable cause. This means you have a reasonable belief, based on particular facts, that evidence of a crime is present within the vehicle.

Here are some scenarios where probable cause for a vehicle search might exist:

• Evidence in plain view: If, during the traffic stop, you observe contraband or evidence of a crime within the vehicle (e.g., drugs, weapons, open containers of alcohol), this constitutes probable cause for a search.

- Odor of illicit substances: The pungent odour of marijuana or other narcotics emanating from the vehicle can be probable cause for a search, as it suggests the presence of illegal drugs.

- Admission of guilt: If the driver admits to possessing illegal substances or weapons within the vehicle, this is a clear justification for a search.

- Outstanding warrant: A warrant for the driver's arrest or a search warrant for the specific vehicle can be grounds for a search.

- Suspicious behaviour: While not enough on its own, erratic driving, nervousness, or attempts to conceal items can be considered alongside other factors to establish probable cause.

It's crucial to remember:

- Search scope: The scope of your search should be limited to the area where you have probable cause to believe evidence exists. Searching for a broken taillight doesn't justify searching the entire vehicle for drugs.

- Inventory search: If a vehicle is being impounded, you can conduct a standardized inventory search to protect the vehicle's contents and identify any valuables for safekeeping.

- Search warrants: If you lack probable cause but have reasonable suspicion, you might seek a warrant from a judge to authorize a more extensive search.

Documenting your actions is essential. Clearly articulate the reason for the search, the facts that established probable cause, and the scope of the search conducted. Remember, conducting lawful vehicle searches requires a strong understanding of your authority and a commitment to upholding citizens' rights.

INVESTIGATING SUSPICIOUS PERSONS

Identifying indicators of suspicious behaviour: reading between the lines

A keen eye for detail is crucial for self-mounted patrol officers. Identifying indicators of suspicious behaviour allows you to proactively investigate potential criminal activity and deter crime before it occurs. Here are some key behaviours to watch for:

• Individuals: People acting nervous, out of place, or loitering around closed businesses at unusual hours might warrant further investigation. Look for erratic behaviour, attempts to conceal themselves, or excessive focus on your patrol car.

• Inconsistencies: Pay attention to inconsistencies in a person's story or demeanour. Someone who seems vague about their reason for being in a particular location or provides conflicting information could be hiding something.

• Criminal activity: Be observant of activities that might suggest criminal intent, such as someone casing a store, trying to open car doors, or carrying known burglary tools.

- Unusual activity: Consider the context. Someone acting strangely in a high-traffic area might not be suspicious, but the same behaviour in a deserted alley at night could be a cause for concern.

Remember, not all suspicious behaviour indicates criminal activity. However, it's your responsibility to investigate further. Here's how to approach a potential suspect:

- Maintain a safe distance: Never put yourself at unnecessary risk. Maintain a safe distance and approach with caution, especially if the person is acting erratically.

- Verbal communication: Engage the person in a polite but firm manner. Ask them to explain their presence and reason for acting suspiciously. Observe their body language and responses for inconsistencies.

- Request identification: If you have reasonable suspicion that the person is involved in criminal activity, you can request identification. This allows you to verify their identity and check for outstanding warrants.

By recognizing these indicators and taking a measured approach to interacting with suspicious persons, you can effectively deter crime and maintain a safe and secure community. Remember, even seemingly insignificant details can be crucial clues, so don't hesitate to investigate when your intuition raises a red flag.

Approaching and questioning individuals: De-escalation and information gathering

Encountering suspicious individuals is a routine part of self-mounted patrol. While maintaining officer safety is paramount, effectively approaching and questioning these individuals is crucial for gathering information and potentially deterring criminal activity.

Here's how to navigate this interaction:

- Prioritize safety: Always assess the situation before approaching. If the person appears armed, erratic, or potentially violent, request backup immediately. Maintain a safe distance and consider your surroundings for potential cover.

- Professional demeanour: Project a calm and professional demeanour throughout the interaction. Avoid aggressive posturing or sudden movements that could be misconstrued as a threat.

- Clear communication: Introduce yourself as a police officer and explain the reason for approaching them. Use clear and concise language, avoiding jargon or technical terms.

- Active listening: Ask open-ended questions that encourage the person to explain their presence and actions. Listen actively, paying attention to both verbal and nonverbal cues.

De-escalation techniques are essential:

- Non-threatening body language: Maintain a relaxed posture and avoid making eye contact that feels overly assertive.

- Empathy and understanding: Acknowledge their perspective, even if you disagree. Phrases like "I understand you might be nervous, but..." can go a long way.

- Focus on facts: Focus on gathering objective information such as their name, reason for being in the area, and identification (if applicable). Avoid accusatory language or leading questions.

Documenting the encounter is essential:

- Detailed notes: Record the date, time, location, and a detailed description of the individual. Note their physical appearance, clothing, and any identifying features.

- The nature of the interaction: Document the conversation, including the questions you asked and the person's responses. Note any inconsistencies or suspicious behaviour.

By prioritizing safety, clear communication, and active listening, you can effectively approach and question suspicious individuals.

Remember, de-escalation techniques and a focus on gathering facts will help you navigate these situations while ensuring your safety and potentially uncovering valuable information.

Field identification procedures (FIPs) and stop-and-frisk tactics: balancing officer safety with individual rights

Field Identification Procedures (FIPs) and stop-and-frisk tactics are two distinct but interrelated tools available to officers in specific situations. Understanding the legal guidelines and proper application is crucial for both officer safety and protecting citizens' rights.

- Field Identification Procedures (FIPs): FIPs allow officers to request an individual's name and identification during a lawful encounter, such as investigating suspicious activity.

The purpose is to identify the person and potentially check for outstanding warrants.

• Stop-and-frisk tactics: A stop-and-frisk differs from an FIP. It involves a brief, investigatory detention based on reasonable suspicion that the individual is armed and dangerous. A frisk is a limited pat-down of the outer clothing to locate weapons that could harm the officer or others.

Here's what justifies a stop-and-frisk:

• Reasonable suspicion: The officer must have a reasonable suspicion, based on articulable facts, that the individual is armed and dangerous. Hunches or mere curiosity are not sufficient grounds.

• Specific and articulable facts: The officer needs to be able to articulate the specific facts that led them to believe the person is armed and dangerous.

• Limited pat-down: The frisk must be focused on the officer's safety and limited to the outer clothing to locate weapons.

Both FIPs and stop-and-frisk tactics require adherence to specific legal guidelines. Here are some key points to remember:

• Non-discriminatory application: These procedures must be applied in a non-discriminatory manner.

- Officer safety: The primary justification for a stop-and-frisk is officer safety.

- Documentation: Officers need to document the justification for the stop, frisk, and any findings.

Remember: The goal is to strike a balance between officer safety and an individual's right to be free from unreasonable search and seizure. By following proper procedures and utilizing these tactics judiciously, you can ensure your safety while upholding the law.

Recognizing potential mental health situations: when intuition meets training

While patrolling, you might encounter individuals exhibiting behaviours that suggest a potential mental health situation. Being observant and recognizing these signs can help you de-escalate situations, provide appropriate assistance, and potentially connect them with the resources they need. Here's what to watch for:

- Unusual behaviour: People acting erratically, talking to themselves incoherently, or displaying drastic mood swings might be experiencing a mental health crisis. Look for signs of confusion, paranoia, or emotional distress.

- Self-harm or threats of harm: Individuals expressing suicidal thoughts, making threats of violence to themselves or others, or carrying objects that could be used for self-harm require immediate attention.

- Disconnection from reality: People experiencing hallucinations or delusions, appearing unaware of their surroundings, or exhibiting illogical thought patterns might be in a state of mental crisis.

- Substance abuse: While not always indicative of a mental health issue, signs of intoxication or drug use can exacerbate existing mental health conditions and pose a safety risk.

It's important to remember that not everyone exhibiting these behaviours is experiencing a mental health crisis. However, your awareness can be crucial. Here's how to approach the situation:

- Maintain a safe distance: Your safety is paramount. If the person appears agitated or potentially violent, keep a safe distance and request backup from officers trained in de-escalation techniques.

- Calm and empathetic communication: If the situation allows, use calm and empathetic language. Avoid accusatory language or making sudden movements that could be perceived as threatening.

- Focus on de-escalation: The primary goal is to de-escalate the situation and avoid provoking further agitation. Listen actively and try to understand their perspective.

- Offer resources: If appropriate, offer to connect them with mental health resources or emergency medical services.

Recognizing potential mental health situations equips you to respond with compassion and care. By working with mental health professionals and utilizing available resources, you can make a positive difference in the lives of individuals experiencing a crisis.

ARRESTS AND USE OF FORCE

Apprehension techniques and handcuffing procedures: taking control safely

Arresting a suspect requires a measured approach that prioritizes officer safety and control. Apprehension techniques and proper handcuffing procedures are essential for ensuring a safe and controlled arrest for both the officer and the suspect.

Apprehension techniques focus on gaining control of the suspect with minimal force. Here are some key principles:

- Officer positioning: Maintain a position of advantage throughout the arrest. This might involve controlling the suspect's arms from behind or using techniques to take them to the ground safely.

- Verbal commands: Use clear, concise, and firm verbal commands to direct the suspect's movements. Repeat commands as necessary and explain your actions to minimize confusion.

- De-escalation: Whenever possible, prioritize de-escalation tactics. Try to calm the suspect and gain their cooperation before resorting to force.

Handcuffing procedures should be applied swiftly and securely once control is established. Here's what to remember:

- Proper fit: Handcuffs should be snug but not excessively tight, allowing for circulation but preventing slipping.

- Double-locking: Double-check that both handcuffs are securely locked to prevent escape attempts.

- Documenting the arrest: Record the location of the handcuffs on the suspect's body and any injuries sustained during the arrest process.

Remember, using force is always a last resort. Law enforcement officers have a duty to protect themselves and others, but excessive force is never justified. Here are some additional considerations:

- Proportionality of force: The level of force used should be proportional to the suspect's resistance.

- Alternatives to force: Always consider alternative methods of control before resorting to physical force.

- Debriefing: After an arrest involving any use of force, a debriefing with a supervisor is essential to review the actions taken and ensure adherence to protocols.

By mastering these apprehension techniques and handcuffing procedures, you can ensure safe and controlled arrests and minimize the risk of injury to yourself, the suspect, and bystanders. Remember, using force effectively requires proper training and a commitment to using it only when absolutely necessary.

De-escalation strategies during arrests: prioritizing a peaceful resolution

While an arrest might be necessary to apprehend a suspect, a peaceful resolution is always preferable. De-escalation strategies are crucial tools for minimizing the use of force and ensuring the safety of everyone involved. Here's how to prioritize de-escalation during an arrest:

- Maintain a calm and professional demeanour: Projecting calmness helps to de-fuse tension and encourages cooperation. Avoid aggressive posturing, yelling, or making threats.

- Clear and concise communication: Use clear and concise language to explain the situation and your expectations. Avoid jargon or technical terms that could confuse the suspect.

- Active listening: Listen actively to the suspect's concerns and try to understand their perspective. Acknowledge their feelings without condoning their actions.

- Offer a way out. If possible, offer the suspect a way to comply with the arrest peacefully. This might involve giving them a chance to surrender weapons or calm down before physically apprehending them.

- Separate the person from the problem: Focus on apprehending the suspect for the crime, not punishing them on the spot. Avoid making accusatory statements or using derogatory language.

De-escalation techniques are particularly important when dealing with:

- Individuals in crisis: People experiencing mental health issues or emotional distress might require a more patient and empathetic approach.

- Subjects under the influence: Intoxicated individuals might be less responsive to reason, so a calm and clear approach is essential.

- Non-violent suspects: If the suspect is not posing a physical threat, prioritize de-escalation tactics before resorting to force.

Remember, de-escalation is an ongoing process.

Even after gaining initial control, continue to use calming communication and avoid unnecessary actions that could provoke further resistance. Here's what to do if de-escalation fails:

- Request backup: If the situation becomes volatile, don't hesitate to request backup from other officers trained in de-escalation tactics.

- Use of force as a last resort: If de-escalation fails and the suspect poses a threat to themselves or others, use force only as a last resort and within the department's guidelines.

By prioritizing de-escalation strategies during arrests, you can create a safer environment for everyone involved. Remember, a successful arrest doesn't always involve physical force - using your communication skills and empathy can often lead to a peaceful resolution.

Legal justification and documentation of the use of force: transparency and accountability

The use of force is a serious matter with significant legal implications. Understanding legal justification and thorough documentation is essential for officers involved in situations requiring force.

The legal justification for using force rests on two key principles:

- Self-defense or defence of others: Officers have the right to use force to protect themselves or others from imminent harm. This includes situations where the suspect is actively resisting arrest or poses a threat with a weapon.

- Overcoming resistance to arrest: A reasonable amount of force can be used to overcome a suspect's resistance during a lawful arrest. However, the level of force used must be proportional to the level of resistance offered.

Here's what constitutes excessive force:

- Force exceeding the threat: Using more force than necessary to subdue the suspect or prevent harm is considered excessive.

- Force used for retaliation or punishment: Force is a tool for control, not punishment. Using excessive force after the threat is neutralized is illegal.

Thorough documentation is crucial after any use of force incident:

- Detailed narrative: Write a clear and concise report outlining the events leading up to the use of force, the specific actions taken, and the justification for using force. Include details about the suspect's resistance and any injuries sustained.

- Witness statements: If there were any witnesses to the incident, obtain their statements and contact information. Their accounts can be crucial evidence.

- Body-worn camera footage: If available, review body-worn camera footage of the incident and ensure it's properly stored and documented as evidence.

Transparency and accountability are paramount. Detailed documentation ensures that the use of force was justified and applied within legal guidelines. Here's what to remember:

- Departmental review: All use of force incidents will undergo a departmental review process to ensure adherence to protocols.

- Potential legal action: In some cases, the use of force might lead to legal proceedings. Clear documentation protects you and provides a factual record of the events.

By understanding legal justification and prioritizing thorough documentation, you can uphold the law while protecting yourself and ensuring accountability in situations requiring the use of force.

Reporting and after-action review of arrest procedures: learning from every encounter

Following an arrest, a comprehensive reporting and review process is essential. This ensures transparency, identifies areas for improvement, and helps officers learn from their experiences.

Reporting procedures provide a clear and accurate account of the arrest:

- Initial arrest report: This detailed report outlines the events leading up to the arrest, the suspect's behaviour, the charges filed, and any use of force employed. It should include witness statements and details on the evidence collected.

- Use of force report: If force was used during the arrest, a separate report is required. This report should meticulously document the justification for using force, the specific tactics employed, and the level of resistance encountered.

After-action review (AAR) takes this process a step further:

• Debriefing with supervisor: Following an arrest, especially one involving a critical incident or use of force, debrief with a supervisor. Discuss your actions, decision-making process, and any challenges encountered.

• Group AAR: In some cases, a formal AAR might be conducted involving multiple officers who witnessed or participated in the arrest. This allows for a collaborative review of the events and identification of best practices.

The AAR process focuses on:

• Effectiveness of tactics: Analyze whether the arrest procedures used were effective in safely apprehending the suspect and minimizing risk.

• Communication and de-escalation: Evaluate the effectiveness of communication and de-escalation tactics during the arrest.

• Learning opportunities: Identify areas where procedures or training could be improved to enhance future encounters.

By actively participating in these reporting and review processes, you contribute to:

• Transparency and accountability: Detailed reports ensure proper oversight and hold officers accountable for their actions.

• Professional development: After-action reviews provide valuable learning opportunities for officers to refine their skills and tactics.

• Improved policies and procedures: Insights gained from AARs can inform policy updates and training enhancements to prepare officers for future situations better.

Through comprehensive reporting and a commitment to learning from each arrest, you can continuously refine your approach and ensure your own safety, that of the public, and that of those being apprehended.

CRIME SCENE MANAGEMENT

Securing and isolating the crime scene: preserving a pristine picture

The initial steps taken at a crime scene are crucial for a successful investigation. Securing and isolating the scene is paramount to maintaining evidence and ensuring a thorough reconstruction of events. Here's how to establish a secure and controlled environment:

• Rapid response: Upon arrival at a crime scene, prioritize your safety and assess the situation. If necessary, request backup from other officers to assist with securing the perimeter.

• Establish a perimeter: The first step is to create a clearly defined perimeter around the crime scene. This might involve using crime scene tape, cones, or other barriers to restrict access. The size of the perimeter will depend on the nature of the crime but should be large enough to encompass all potential evidence.

- Restrict access: Only authorized personnel, such as investigators, crime scene technicians, and emergency medical personnel (if needed), should be allowed within the perimeter. This minimizes contamination and ensures the integrity of the evidence.

Scene isolation involves meticulous measures:

- Scene entry and exit protocol: Establish a designated entry and exit point for authorized personnel. This allows for control over movement within the scene and minimizes the risk of trampling or disturbing evidence.

- Document entry and exit: Maintain a log of everyone entering and exiting the crime scene, including the time and reason for their presence. This recordkeeping is essential for chain-of-custody documentation.

- Weather control: If possible, take steps to protect the scene from the elements. This might involve setting up a temporary shelter to shield the scene from rain, snow, or excessive sunlight, which can damage or obscure evidence.

Remember, a secure crime scene is a foundation for a successful investigation. By taking these initial steps to isolate and protect the area, you:

- Preserve evidence: Minimizing contamination and disturbance safeguards the integrity of physical evidence crucial for identifying suspects and reconstructing the crime.

- Facilitate investigation: A secure scene allows investigators to work methodically and efficiently, documenting the scene and collecting evidence without disruptions.

- Protect witnesses and bystanders: By restricting access to authorized personnel, you ensure the safety of witnesses and bystanders who might be emotionally distressed or vulnerable.

By prioritizing scene security and isolation, you lay the groundwork for a thorough investigation that can bring justice to the victim and hold perpetrators accountable.

Initial investigation and evidence preservation: building the foundation for a case

Following the crucial steps of securing and isolating the crime scene, the initial investigative phase commences. This stage focuses on gathering preliminary information, identifying potential evidence, and taking steps to preserve it for further analysis. Here's how to lay the groundwork for a strong case:

- Scene assessment: Once the scene is secure, conduct a comprehensive visual survey to identify potential evidence. This might include objects on the ground, marks on surfaces, bloodstains, fingerprints, or anything that seems out of place.

- Witness interviews: If there are any witnesses to the crime, interview them promptly while their memories are fresh. Gather their accounts of the event, including descriptions of the suspect(s), actions, and other relevant details.

- Victim identification and interview: If the crime involved a victim, identify and interview them if possible. Their testimony can be crucial for understanding the events that transpired. Remember to prioritize their well-being and provide support throughout the interview process.

Evidence preservation is paramount:

- Documenting the scene: Meticulously document the crime scene through photographs and detailed notes. Photographs should capture the scene from various angles, including close-up shots of potential evidence. Notes should detail the location and condition of all observed evidence.

- Evidence collection: Properly collect and package any potential evidence once documented. Follow department protocols for handling different types of evidence, such as fingerprints, DNA samples, or ballistic evidence. Minimize contamination by wearing gloves and using appropriate collection materials.

• Chain of custody: Maintain a clear chain of custody for all collected evidence. This documented record tracks the movement of evidence from the crime scene to the laboratory for analysis, ensuring its admissibility in court.

By prioritizing these steps, you contribute to building a strong foundation for the investigation. A thorough initial investigation and meticulous evidence preservation are essential for the following:

• Identifying suspects: Physical evidence can link suspects to the crime scene and support witness testimonies.

• Reconstructing the crime: Evidence analysis can help investigators piece together the sequence of events and understand the perpetrator's motives.

• Securing convictions: Properly collected and documented evidence is crucial for presenting a compelling case in court and securing a conviction.

Remember, the initial investigation sets the stage for the entire case. By meticulously gathering information and preserving evidence, you play a vital role in bringing perpetrators to justice.

Interviewing witnesses and gathering information: unveiling the pieces of the puzzle

Following crime scene security and initial assessment, witness interviews become a cornerstone of a successful investigation.

Extracting accurate and detailed information from witnesses is crucial for piecing together the events. Here's how to conduct effective witness interviews:

• Separate witnesses: Interview witnesses individually to prevent them from influencing each other's accounts. This ensures you obtain their unique perspectives without the risk of contamination.

• Active listening: Create a safe and comfortable space for the witness. Practice active listening, paying close attention to both verbal and nonverbal cues. Encourage them to narrate the events in their own words, avoiding leading questions.

• Open-ended questions: Utilize open-ended questions that prompt the witness to elaborate on their observations. Ask about the suspect's appearance, behaviour, and any details they might recall about the crime itself.

Careful observation goes a long way:

• Nonverbal cues: While listening attentively, pay attention to the witness's body language. Nervousness, hesitation, or inconsistencies in their story can be indicators of potential issues or withheld information.

• Memory jogs: If the witness struggles to recall details, use gentle memory jogs. This might involve showing them photographs from the scene or asking them to retrace their steps if they were present during the crime.

Thorough documentation is essential:

• Detailed notes: Take detailed notes throughout the interview, recording the witness's statements, demeanour, and any inconsistencies observed. Note the date, time, and location of the interview for recordkeeping purposes.

• Witness statements: If the witness is comfortable, obtain a signed written statement summarizing their account of the events. This documented statement can be a valuable reference point throughout the investigation.

Witness interviews are a collaborative effort:

• Building rapport: Establishing rapport with the witness is key. Treat them with respect and empathy, acknowledging the emotional strain they might be experiencing.

- Clarifying information: As the interview progresses, ask clarifying questions to ensure you fully understand their testimony. Avoid interrupting them, but politely seek clarification if needed.

By conducting well-structured witness interviews and meticulously gathering information, you contribute significantly to the investigation.

These accounts, along with physical evidence, provide a comprehensive picture of the crime and pave the way for identifying suspects and building a strong case.

Cooperation with detectives and crime scene technicians: building a cohesive investigative team

A successful crime scene investigation hinges on collaboration. While securing the scene and conducting initial inquiries are crucial first steps, effective teamwork with detectives and crime scene technicians (CSIs) is essential for a thorough investigation.

- Detectives: Detectives are the lead investigators responsible for overseeing the case. They will rely on your observations from the scene and any witness statements you obtain to develop investigative leads.

• Crime Scene Technicians (CSIs): CSIs are specialists trained in meticulous evidence collection and processing. Their expertise is vital for identifying, collecting, and preserving physical evidence that can link suspects to the crime.

Here's how to foster a collaborative environment:

• Clear communication: Maintain clear and consistent communication with detectives and CSIs. Brief them on the scene layout, potential evidence you observed, and any witness interactions you had.

• Scene security: As the first officer on the scene, you are responsible for maintaining scene security until detectives and CSIs arrive. Ensure their unhindered access to the scene while preventing unauthorized personnel from entering.

• Respecting expertise: Recognize the detectives' and CSIs' expertise in their respective fields. Please provide them with all the information you have gathered, but avoid interfering with their specialized tasks.

Collaboration goes beyond the initial response:

• Ongoing communication: As the investigation progresses, detectives might require further details from you or the scene.

Be readily available to answer questions and provide any additional information you might recall.

• Sharing observations: If you encounter new information or potential evidence during your patrol duties that might be relevant to the case, don't hesitate to share it with the detectives.

• Maintaining confidentiality: Remember to maintain confidentiality throughout the investigation. Avoid discussing case details with unauthorized personnel or the public.

Effective collaboration fosters a well-rounded investigation. By working cohesively with detectives and CSIs, you ensure:

• A comprehensive investigation: The combined efforts of patrol officers, detectives, and CSIs lead to a more thorough understanding of the crime.

• Efficient use of resources: Clear communication and defined roles prevent duplication of effort and ensure optimal use of investigative resources.

• Strong case presentation: Collaborative information sharing strengthens the case presented in court by detectives, as it's built on a foundation of comprehensive investigation.

By prioritizing teamwork and respecting each other's expertise, you and your colleagues from various units can work together to solve crimes and ensure justice prevails.

DOMESTIC VIOLENCE INTERVENTION

Recognizing signs of domestic violence: intervening before escalation

Domestic violence is a serious crime that can impact people from all walks of life. Recognizing the signs is crucial for intervening before a situation escalates. Here's what to watch for:

• Physical signs: Look for injuries such as bruises, cuts, or burns. Be aware of attempts to conceal injuries with clothing or makeup.

• Controlling behaviour: A perpetrator might exhibit controlling behaviour, such as monitoring a partner's phone calls, restricting their movements, or dictating their clothing choices.

• Emotional abuse: Verbal threats, insults, intimidation, and humiliation are all signs of emotional abuse. Pay attention to a person appearing withdrawn, fearful, or walking on eggshells around their partner.

- Isolation: The perpetrator might isolate their partner from friends and family, preventing them from having a support system.

Be aware of the following dynamics:

- Imbalance of power: Domestic violence relationships are often characterized by an imbalance of power, with the perpetrator controlling and dominating the victim.

- Cycle of violence: Domestic violence often follows a cycle of tension building, violence, apologies, and a honeymoon phase. Be aware that a seemingly calm period might precede another violent outburst.

Not every situation will present all these signs, but even a few red flags warrant attention. Here's what you can do:

- Confidentiality: Maintain confidentiality unless there's immediate danger. Let the person experiencing violence know you're there to listen and offer resources for help.

- Safety planning: If someone discloses abuse, help them develop a safety plan, such as having a code word for emergencies or identifying a safe place to go.

- Connecting with resources: Provide information on hotlines, shelters, and support groups specializing in domestic violence.

Recognizing signs of domestic violence allows you to:

- Help those in need: By identifying potential victims, you can connect them with resources and support systems that can help them escape a violent situation.

- Prevent future violence: Early intervention can prevent a violent situation from escalating and potentially save lives.

Remember, domestic violence is a complex issue, but by being observant and offering support, you can make a positive difference in the lives of those affected.

De-escalation tactics and victim safety protocols: prioritizing calm and protection

Domestic violence calls require a measured approach that prioritizes both officer safety and the safety of the victim. Here's how to utilize de-escalation tactics and adhere to victim safety protocols during these interventions:

De-escalation tactics are paramount:

- Separate the parties: When responding to a domestic violence call, your primary goal is to separate the individuals involved. This minimizes the risk of further violence and allows you to assess the situation.

- Calm and empathetic communication: Use calm and empathetic language to de-escalate the situation. Avoid accusatory language or yelling, which could further inflame tensions.

- Active listening: Listen actively to both parties, but prioritize the safety of the victim. Validate their fears and concerns, and let them know you're there to help.

Victim safety protocols are essential:

- Lethal danger assessment: Assess the potential for lethal violence. Look for signs like weapons, threats of harm, or a history of violence. If immediate danger exists, prioritize removing the victim to safety and requesting backup.

- Confidentiality and support: Respect the victim's privacy and offer them resources for confidential support. Inform them about their legal options and the availability of shelters or victim advocacy groups.

- Scene documentation: Document the scene thoroughly, including any injuries observed, damage to property, and statements from potential witnesses. This documentation is crucial for potential legal proceedings.

Remember, your role is to intervene, de-escalate, and protect.

Here are some additional considerations:

- Domestic violence cycle: Be aware of the cycle of domestic violence and the potential for future outbursts. Provide the victim with resources for ongoing support and safety planning.

- Children present: If children are present, prioritize their safety as well. Remove them from the scene if possible and connect them with appropriate support services.

- Professional follow-up: Following the intervention, ensure the victim has access to resources and support services. Documenting the incident and maintaining a record is essential for potential follow-up investigations.

By prioritizing de-escalation tactics and adhering to victim safety protocols, you can effectively intervene in domestic violence situations. Your actions can help protect victims, prevent further violence, and connect them with the support they need to break the cycle of abuse.

Apprehension of domestic violence offenders: apprehension of domestic violence offenders

Apprehending a domestic violence offender requires a delicate balance between ensuring the victim's safety and upholding due process. Here's how to navigate this situation effectively:

Prioritizing victim safety:

- Lethal danger assessment: Reassess the potential for lethal danger. If the offender poses a threat to the victim or yourself, immediate apprehension might be necessary to prevent further harm.

- Protective orders: If there are existing restraining orders or protective orders against the offender, their violation could be grounds for arrest. Ensure you have a copy of the order readily available.

- Victim wishes: If possible, consider the victim's wishes regarding the offender's apprehension. While respecting their autonomy, prioritize their safety and advise on the legal options available, such as requesting a restraining order.

Following due process:

- Probable cause: An arrest for domestic violence requires probable cause to believe a crime has been committed. This might involve visible injuries on the victim, witness statements, or a history of domestic violence calls to the exact location.

- Search warrants: If necessary, obtain a search warrant to enter the premises and apprehend the offender, especially if there's a risk of them destroying evidence or harming themselves or others.

- Miranda rights: Once the offender is apprehended, inform them of their Miranda rights, which include the right to remain silent and the right to an attorney.

Collaboration is key:

- Working with detectives: Collaborate with detectives to gather evidence and build a strong case against the offender. This could involve witness statements, medical records of the victim's injuries, and any damaged property at the scene.

- Connecting victim with resources: Reiterate the availability of support services and resources for the victim, such as shelters, legal aid, and counselling. This empowers them to rebuild their lives free from violence.

Apprehending domestic violence offenders is a crucial step in holding them accountable and preventing further harm. However, ensuring victim safety and upholding legal procedures are paramount throughout the process. By prioritizing these principles, you can contribute to a more secure environment for victims and a more just legal outcome.

Reporting and victim support resources: empowering healing and accountability

Following a domestic violence intervention, thorough reporting and connecting victims with support resources are essential next steps. Here's how to ensure a comprehensive response:

Detailed reporting:

• Incident report: File a detailed incident report documenting the events leading up to the intervention. This should include the nature of the violence, any injuries observed, witness statements (if applicable), and the actions taken, including de-escalation tactics and apprehensions (if any).

• Evidence collection: If there is evidence of violence, such as damaged property or weapons, ensure it's collected and documented following department protocols. This evidence can be crucial for building a strong case against the offender.

Connecting victims with support:

• Victim advocacy: Inform the victim about available victim advocacy services. These organizations can provide emotional support, legal guidance, and assistance with safety planning and navigating the legal system.

• Shelter resources: If the victim requires immediate safe haven, provide them with information on local shelters or temporary housing options where they can escape the abusive environment.

• Counseling services: Domestic violence can have lasting emotional and psychological impacts. Connect the victim with counselling services to help them process the trauma and rebuild their well-being.

Here's how these steps contribute to a positive outcome:

• Accountability: Detailed reports and evidence collection are crucial for holding offenders accountable through the legal process.

• Empowering victims: Connecting victims with support resources empowers them to access the help they need to heal from the trauma and rebuild their lives.

• Preventing future violence: By providing ongoing support and safety planning, you can help victims break the cycle of domestic violence and prevent future abuse.

Remember, your role extends beyond the immediate intervention. By ensuring thorough reporting and connecting victims with support resources, you contribute to a comprehensive response that prioritizes both safety and healing in domestic violence situations.

PART 3: PSYCHOLOGICAL ASPECTS AND TEAMWORK

COPING WITH STRESS AND TRAUMA

Understanding the impact of police work on mental health

Police work is a demanding profession that can take a significant toll on mental health. Officers routinely face stressful and traumatic situations, including violence, death, and human suffering. Here's a closer look at how these experiences can impact mental well-being:

- Chronic stress exposure: Police officers are constantly exposed to high-pressure situations, from responding to emergencies to dealing with volatile individuals. This chronic stress can lead to burnout, anxiety, and depression.

- Secondary traumatic stress: Witnessing traumatic events can have a psychological impact, even on those not directly involved. Officers who repeatedly see violence and suffering can experience secondary traumatic stress, similar to PTSD (post-traumatic stress disorder).

- Difficult decisions and moral dilemmas: Police work often involves making split-second decisions with potentially life-altering consequences. The weight of these choices and the moral complexities of certain situations can contribute to emotional strain.

Recognizing the signs of mental health issues is crucial:

- Changes in mood or behavior: Watch for signs of withdrawal, irritability, insomnia, or changes in appetite. These can indicate underlying depression or anxiety.

- Difficulty coping with stress: If an officer seems overwhelmed by everyday situations or struggles to manage stress effectively, it might be a sign of deeper issues.

- Increased substance use: Self-medication through alcohol or drugs can be a coping mechanism for stress and trauma, but it can exacerbate mental health problems in the long run.

By understanding the impact of police work on mental health, you can:

- Reduce stigma: Openly acknowledging the challenges officers face can help reduce the stigma associated with seeking mental health help.

- Promote help-seeking behavior: Encourage officers to prioritize their mental well-being and create a supportive environment where seeking help is seen as a strength, not a weakness.

- Develop resilience: Training programs that promote stress management techniques and emotional intelligence can help officers build resilience and cope with challenging situations more effectively.

Recognizing the mental health challenges faced by police officers is vital for creating a healthier and more sustainable work environment. By taking proactive steps and promoting help-seeking behavior, we can ensure officers receive the support they need to maintain their well-being and continue serving their communities effectively.

Techniques for stress management and emotional resilience: building inner strength

The demanding nature of police work necessitates effective strategies for managing stress and building emotional resilience. Here are some techniques officers can incorporate into their daily lives:

- Mindfulness and relaxation practices: Techniques like meditation, deep breathing exercises, and progressive muscle relaxation can help calm the nervous system and promote feelings of peace and focus. Regularly practicing mindfulness allows officers to become more aware of their thoughts and emotions, enabling them to respond constructively instead of reacting impulsively.

- Physical activity: Regular exercise is a powerful tool for managing stress and improving overall well-being. Engaging in activities they enjoy, whether individual workouts or team sports, can help officers release tension, boost endorphins, and improve sleep quality – all contributing factors to emotional resilience.

- Healthy lifestyle choices: Maintaining a balanced diet, getting adequate sleep, and limiting alcohol and caffeine consumption are essential for physical and mental health. Prioritizing these choices helps officers feel energized and better equipped to handle the demands of the job.

Building a strong support system is equally important:

- Confiding in colleagues: Having a network of supportive colleagues who understand the challenges of police work can be a source of strength and comfort.

Sharing experiences and emotions with trusted peers can help officers feel less alone and provide valuable perspectives.

- Seeking professional help: Therapy can be a valuable tool for managing stress, coping with trauma, and developing coping mechanisms. Encouraging officers to seek professional help when needed demonstrates a commitment to their well-being and ensures they have the resources to thrive.

By incorporating these techniques, officers can:

- Reduce stress levels: Effective stress management techniques equip officers with tools to regulate their emotions and maintain a sense of calm in demanding situations.

- Enhance emotional resilience: Building emotional resilience allows officers to bounce back from setbacks and challenges they encounter in the line of duty.

- Maintain perspective: Strong coping mechanisms allow officers to maintain a healthy perspective on their experiences, preventing them from becoming overwhelmed by stress or trauma.

Investing in stress management and emotional resilience empowers police officers to navigate the challenges of their profession while maintaining their mental well-being. This, in turn, fosters a healthier and more resilient workforce that can effectively serve and protect their communities.

Critical incident stress debriefing (CISD) resources: processing trauma as a team

Following critical incidents, officers may experience emotional distress, confusion, or difficulty processing the events. Critical Incident Stress Debriefing (CISD) resources offer a structured approach to navigate these challenges.

What is CISD?

CISD is a group intervention facilitated by a trained mental health professional. It provides officers with a safe and confidential space to discuss their experiences, share their reactions, and receive support from colleagues who understand the emotional impact of such events.

Benefits of CISD:

- Normalization of reactions: CISD helps officers realize that their feelings are normal responses to abnormal events. Sharing experiences with peers who have been through similar situations can alleviate feelings of isolation and guilt.

- Emotional processing: The debriefing process allows officers to verbalize their thoughts and emotions, promoting healthy emotional processing and preventing the development of long-term psychological issues.

- Coping skills development: CISD sessions can equip officers with coping skills and strategies for managing stress and trauma in the aftermath of critical incidents.

Accessing CISD Resources:

- Departmental programs: Many police departments have in-house CISD programs or collaborate with mental health professionals to provide these services to officers following critical incidents.

- Peer support programs: Peer support programs connect officers with colleagues who have undergone specialized training to provide emotional support and guidance.

- Employee Assistance Programs (EAPs): Many departments offer EAPs that provide confidential counseling services to officers dealing with stress, trauma, or personal challenges.

Remember, seeking help is a sign of strength. Utilizing CISD resources demonstrates a proactive approach to mental health and emotional well-being. By taking advantage of these services, officers can process difficult experiences, build resilience, and return to duty feeling supported and empowered.

Maintaining a healthy work-life balance: fueling your well-being

The demanding nature of police work can easily tip the scales towards work dominating an officer's life. However, maintaining a healthy work-life balance is crucial for sustained well-being and optimal performance on the job. Here are some strategies to achieve this balance:

- Setting boundaries: Establish clear boundaries between work and personal life. Disconnect from work emails and calls during off-duty hours to create dedicated time for relaxation and rejuvenation.

- Prioritizing personal interests: Make time for hobbies, social activities, and spending quality time with loved ones. Engaging in activities they enjoy allows officers to recharge emotionally and maintain a sense of perspective outside of work.

- Scheduling time for self-care: Prioritize activities that promote physical and mental well-being. This could include getting enough sleep, practicing relaxation techniques, or engaging in activities that bring joy and reduce stress.

Effective time management is key:

- Planning and organization: Develop a schedule that balances work commitments with personal time. Planning ahead and prioritizing tasks can help officers manage workload efficiently and avoid feeling overwhelmed.

- Delegation when possible: Learning to delegate tasks appropriately within the department can free up valuable time for officers to focus on high-priority matters and reduce their overall workload.

- Saying no: It's okay to decline additional work assignments if it jeopardizes personal well-being. Setting boundaries and advocating for their time allows officers to maintain a healthy work-life balance.

The benefits of a healthy work-life balance are numerous:

- Reduced stress levels: Disconnecting from work allows officers to de-stress and return to their duties feeling refreshed and more focused.

- Improved job performance: A well-rested and emotionally balanced officer is better equipped to handle challenging situations and make sound decisions.

- Stronger relationships: Prioritizing time for loved ones strengthens personal connections and provides a strong support system outside of work.

Remember, a healthy work-life balance is an investment in your overall well-being. By incorporating these strategies and advocating for their time, officers can create a sustainable career path that allows them to serve their communities effectively while prioritizing their physical and mental health.

THE IMPORTANCE OF PARTNERSHIP

Effective communication and collaboration with patrol partner: building a cohesive unit

A patrol partner is more than just a colleague; they are your confidant, backup, and teammate in the field. Effective communication and collaboration with your partner are essential for ensuring officer safety, efficient problem-solving, and fostering a positive work environment.

Communication is key:

- Clear and concise communication: Develop a clear and concise communication style with your partner. This includes verbal communication during calls, as well as non-verbal cues that signal potential hazards or intentions.

- Active listening: Practice active listening, paying close attention to your partner's updates, observations, and concerns. Acknowledge their input and ensure they feel heard and valued.

- Pre-call briefings: Establish a routine for brief pre-call discussions. Quickly share information about the nature of the call, potential risks, and a plan of action to approach the situation collaboratively.

Collaboration builds a stronger team:

- Shared roles and responsibilities: Clearly define shared roles and responsibilities during patrols. This could involve one officer taking point on traffic stops while the other focuses on crowd control at an event, ensuring a coordinated response.

- Mutual trust and respect: Develop a foundation of mutual trust and respect with your partner. Knowing you can rely on your partner's skills and judgment fosters confidence and a sense of security during patrols.

- Anticipating each other's needs: Over time, you'll develop an understanding of each other's strengths and weaknesses. Learn to anticipate your partner's needs and anticipate situations where they might require backup or support.

Effective communication and collaboration benefit everyone:

- Enhanced officer safety: Clear communication and a shared understanding of situations minimize confusion and allow for coordinated responses, ultimately enhancing officer safety.

- Improved problem-solving: Working together as a team allows you to leverage each other's strengths and perspectives, leading to more effective problem-solving and decision-making during critical incidents.

- Positive work environment: A strong partnership fosters a sense of camaraderie and support, making challenging situations more manageable and fostering a more positive work environment.

By prioritizing clear communication, collaboration, and mutual respect, you and your patrol partner can build a cohesive unit that effectively serves and protects the community.

Recognizing signs of stress and supporting your partner: a pillar of partnership

The demanding nature of police work can take a toll on anyone. As partners, you not only share the workload but also become keenly aware of each other's well-being. Recognizing the signs of stress in your partner and offering support is a crucial aspect of a strong partnership.

Signs of stress to watch for:

- Changes in behavior: Notice any significant changes in your partner's behavior, such as increased irritability, withdrawal from social interaction, or difficulty concentrating.

- Physical manifestations: Stress can manifest physically through changes in sleep patterns, appetite, or a higher frequency of headaches or stomachaches.

- Emotional cues: Pay attention to emotional cues like frustration, anger outbursts, or a sense of detachment.

Offering support and building resilience:

- Open communication: Maintain open communication and create a safe space for your partner to express their concerns without judgment. Listen actively and offer empathy.

- Practical support: Look for ways to offer practical support during particularly stressful periods. This could involve covering some workload, helping with paperwork, or simply offering to run errands.

- Encouraging help-seeking: If your partner is struggling to cope, gently encourage them to seek professional help. Offer to accompany them to therapy appointments or help them research resources.

Remember, you're not a therapist, but you can be a source of strength:

- Active listening: Sometimes, all your partner needs is a listening ear and someone to validate their feelings. Active listening demonstrates your support and can be a powerful tool for emotional processing.

- Positive reinforcement: Acknowledge your partner's resilience and coping mechanisms. Positive reinforcement can help them feel more confident in their ability to handle stress.

- Self-care reminder: Gently remind your partner of the importance of self-care. Encourage them to prioritize healthy sleep, exercise, and activities they enjoy to manage stress effectively.

By recognizing the signs of stress and offering support, you become a pillar of strength for your partner. This fosters a strong working relationship built on mutual trust and respect, allowing you to navigate challenges together and ensure each other's well-being throughout your service.

Building trust and mutual respect within the partnership: the foundation of success

The foundation of any successful police partnership is built on a bedrock of trust and mutual respect. These qualities go beyond simple courtesy and create a working environment where officers feel confident, supported, and empowered to perform their duties effectively.

Here's how to cultivate trust and respect within your partnership:

- Open and honest communication: Maintain open and honest communication with your partner. Share your observations, concerns, and even mistakes in a transparent manner. Being upfront fosters trust and allows for collaborative problem-solving.

- Acknowledging strengths and weaknesses: Recognize and appreciate each other's strengths and weaknesses. Understanding these differences allows you to rely on each other's expertise and compensate for areas where one might need support.

- Respecting boundaries: Respect your partner's boundaries, both professional and personal. This includes respecting their preferred communication styles, work habits, and need for personal space during patrols.

Actions speak louder than words:

- Reliability and dependability: Always strive to be reliable and dependable for your partner. Knowing they can count on you in any situation builds trust and fosters a sense of security.

- Active listening and empathy: Practice active listening and demonstrate empathy towards your partner's experiences and challenges. Show genuine interest in their well-being and offer support when needed.

- Shared decision-making: Whenever possible, involve your partner in decision-making processes. Consider their perspectives and value their input, fostering a sense of shared responsibility and ownership over the work you do together.

The benefits of trust and mutual respect are numerous:

- Enhanced officer safety: Knowing you can trust your partner to have your back in any situation allows for more coordinated responses and ultimately enhances officer safety.

- Improved problem-solving: Working as a team with mutual respect allows you to leverage each other's strengths and perspectives, leading to more effective problem-solving and better outcomes.

- Positive work environment: A partnership built on trust and respect fosters a positive work environment where officers feel comfortable, valued, and motivated to perform their best.

By prioritizing open communication, acknowledging individual strengths, and demonstrating respect, you and your partner can build an unbreakable bond. This foundation of trust and mutual respect will empower you to face any challenge together, ensuring a successful and fulfilling partnership.

Utilizing each other's strengths for optimal results: a team advantage

The success of a police partnership hinges not just on trust and respect, but also on capitalizing on each other's strengths. By recognizing and leveraging your partner's unique skills and experiences, you can create a formidable team that delivers optimal results.

Identifying individual strengths:

- Self-awareness: Be introspective about your own strengths and weaknesses. What are you particularly skilled at? In what areas could you benefit from your partner's expertise?

- Open communication: Openly discuss each other's strengths and areas for development. This allows you to assign tasks and approach situations in a way that optimizes your combined skillset.

- Past experiences: Consider your partner's background and past experiences. They might have expertise in de-escalation tactics, crisis intervention, or specific aspects of criminal investigation.

Optimizing performance through collaboration:

- Task delegation: Delegate tasks based on strengths. If your partner excels at building rapport with civilians, they might take point during community interactions, while you handle tasks requiring strong analytical skills.

- Complementary skillsets: Recognize how your strengths complement each other. A more assertive partner might take the lead in high-pressure situations, while a more patient officer can provide a calming influence.

- Continuous learning: Be open to learning from each other. If your partner excels in a particular area, ask them to share their knowledge and expertise. This fosters mutual growth and strengthens your teamwork.

The benefits of leveraging strengths are numerous:

- Enhanced problem-solving: By combining your areas of expertise, you can approach problems from multiple angles, leading to more creative and effective solutions.

- Improved efficiency: Delegation based on strengths allows you to work more efficiently, completing tasks quickly and accurately.

- Increased confidence: Knowing you have a partner who complements your skillset fosters confidence in your abilities to handle any situation that arises.

Remember, a strong partnership is more than the sum of its parts. By recognizing each other's strengths and working together effectively, you can create a team that delivers exceptional results while fostering a sense of accomplishment and shared purpose in your police work.

LEGAL CONSIDERATIONS AND REPORT WRITING

Understanding relevant laws and department policies: a foundation for effective action

Police work is a demanding profession that can take a significant toll on mental health. Officers routinely face stressful and traumatic situations, including violence, death, and human suffering. Here's a closer look at how these experiences can impact mental well-being:

• Chronic stress exposure: Police officers are constantly exposed to high-pressure situations, from responding to emergencies to dealing with volatile individuals. This chronic stress can lead to burnout, anxiety, and depression.

• Secondary traumatic stress: Witnessing traumatic events can have a psychological impact, even on those not directly involved. Officers who repeatedly see violence and suffering can experience secondary traumatic stress, similar to PTSD (post-traumatic stress disorder).

• Difficult decisions and moral dilemmas: Police work often involves making split-second decisions with potentially life-altering consequences. The weight of these choices and the moral complexities of certain situations can contribute to emotional strain.

Recognizing the signs of mental health issues is crucial:

• Changes in mood or behaviour: Watch for signs of withdrawal, irritability, insomnia, or changes in appetite. These can indicate underlying depression or anxiety.

• Difficulty coping with stress: If an officer seems overwhelmed by everyday situations or struggles to manage stress effectively, it might be a sign of deeper issues.

• Increased substance use: Self-medication through alcohol or drugs can be a coping mechanism for stress and trauma, but it can exacerbate mental health problems in the long run.

By understanding the impact of police work on mental health, you can:

• Reduce stigma: Openly acknowledging the challenges officers face can help reduce the stigma associated with seeking mental health help.

- Promote help-seeking behaviour: Encourage officers to prioritize their mental well-being and create a supportive environment where seeking help is seen as a strength, not a weakness.

- Develop resilience: Training programs that promote stress management techniques and emotional intelligence can help officers build resilience and cope with challenging situations more effectively.

Recognizing the mental health challenges faced by police officers is vital for creating a healthier and more sustainable work environment. By taking proactive steps and promoting help-seeking behaviour, we can ensure officers receive the support they need to maintain their well-being and continue serving their communities effectively.

Techniques for stress management and emotional resilience: building inner strength

The demanding nature of police work necessitates effective strategies for managing stress and building emotional resilience. Here are some techniques officers can incorporate into their daily lives:

- Mindfulness and relaxation practices: Techniques like meditation, deep breathing exercises, and progressive muscle relaxation can help calm the nervous system and promote feelings of peace and focus. Regularly practising mindfulness allows officers to become more aware of their thoughts and emotions, enabling them to respond constructively instead of reacting impulsively.

- Physical activity: Regular exercise is a powerful tool for managing stress and improving overall well-being. Engaging in activities they enjoy, whether individual workouts or team sports, can help officers release tension, boost endorphins, and enhance the quality of sleep – all contributing factors to emotional resilience.

- Healthy lifestyle choices: Maintaining a balanced diet, getting adequate sleep, and limiting alcohol and caffeine consumption are essential for physical and mental health. Prioritizing these choices helps officers feel energized and better equipped to handle the demands of the job.

Building a solid support system is equally important:

- Confiding in colleagues: Having a network of supportive colleagues who understand the challenges of police work can be a source of strength and comfort. Sharing experiences and emotions with trusted peers can help officers feel less alone and provide valuable perspectives.

- Seeking professional help: Therapy can be a valuable tool for managing stress, coping with trauma, and developing coping mechanisms. Encouraging officers to seek professional help demonstrates a commitment to their well-being and ensures they have the resources to thrive.

By incorporating these techniques, officers can:

- Reduce stress levels: Effective stress management techniques equip officers with tools to regulate their emotions and maintain a sense of calm in demanding situations.

- Enhance emotional resilience: Building emotional resilience allows officers to bounce back from setbacks and challenges in the line of duty.

- Maintain perspective: Strong coping mechanisms allow officers to maintain a healthy perspective on their experiences, preventing them from becoming overwhelmed by stress or trauma.

Investing in stress management and emotional resilience empowers police officers to navigate the challenges of their profession while maintaining their mental well-being. This, in turn, fosters a healthier and more resilient workforce that can effectively serve and protect their communities.

Critical incident stress debriefing (CISD) resources: processing trauma as a team

Following critical incidents, officers may experience emotional distress, confusion, or difficulty processing the events. Critical Incident Stress Debriefing (CISD) resources offer a structured approach to navigating these challenges.

What is CISD?

CISD is a group intervention facilitated by a trained mental health professional. It provides officers with a safe and confidential space to discuss their experiences, share their reactions, and receive support from colleagues who understand the emotional impact of such events.

Benefits of CISD:

• Normalization of reactions: CISD helps officers realize that their feelings are normal responses to abnormal events. Sharing experiences with peers who have been through similar situations can alleviate feelings of isolation and guilt.

• Emotional processing: The debriefing process allows officers to verbalize their thoughts and emotions, promoting healthy emotional processing and preventing the development of long-term psychological issues.

- Coping skills development: CISD sessions can equip officers with coping skills and strategies for managing stress and trauma in the aftermath of critical incidents.

Accessing CISD Resources:

- Departmental programs: Many police departments have in-house CISD programs or collaborate with mental health professionals to provide these services to officers following critical incidents.

- Peer support programs: Peer support programs connect officers with colleagues who have undergone specialized training to provide emotional support and guidance.

- Employee Assistance Programs (EAPs): Many departments offer EAPs that provide confidential counselling services to officers dealing with stress, trauma, or personal challenges.

Remember, seeking help is a sign of strength.

Utilizing CISD resources demonstrates a proactive approach to mental health and emotional well-being. By taking advantage of these services, officers can process difficult experiences, build resilience, and return to duty feeling supported and empowered.

Maintaining a healthy work-life balance: fueling your well-being

The demanding nature of police work can easily tip the scales towards work dominating an officer's life. However, maintaining a healthy work-life balance is crucial for sustained well-being and optimal performance on the job. Here are some strategies to achieve this balance:

• Setting boundaries: Establish clear boundaries between work and personal life. Disconnect from work emails and calls during off-duty hours to create dedicated time for relaxation and rejuvenation.

• Prioritizing personal interests: Make time for hobbies, social activities, and spending quality time with loved ones. Engaging in activities they enjoy allows officers to recharge emotionally and maintain a sense of perspective outside of work.

• Scheduling time for self-care: Prioritize activities that promote physical and mental well-being. This could include getting enough sleep, practising relaxation techniques, or engaging in activities that bring joy and reduce stress.

Effective time management is key:

- Planning and organization: Develop a schedule that balances work commitments with personal time. Planning ahead and prioritizing tasks can help officers manage their workload efficiently and avoid feeling overwhelmed.

- Delegation when possible: Learning to delegate tasks appropriately within the department can free up valuable time for officers to focus on high-priority matters and reduce their overall workload.

- Saying no: Decreasing additional work assignments is okay if it jeopardizes personal well-being. Setting boundaries and advocating for their time allows officers to maintain a healthy work-life balance.

The benefits of a healthy work-life balance are numerous:

- Reduced stress levels: Disconnecting from work allows officers to de-stress and return to their duties feeling refreshed and more focused.

- Improved job performance: A well-rested and emotionally balanced officer is better equipped to handle challenging situations and make sound decisions.

- Stronger relationships: Prioritizing time for loved ones strengthens personal connections and provides a strong support system outside of work.

Remember, a healthy work-life balance is an investment in your overall well-being. By incorporating these strategies and advocating for their time, officers can create a sustainable career path that allows them to serve their communities effectively while prioritizing their physical and mental health.

THE IMPORTANCE OF PARTNERSHIP

Effective communication and collaboration with patrol partner: building a cohesive unit

A patrol partner is more than just a colleague; they are your confidant, backup, and teammate in the field. Effective communication and collaboration with your partner are essential for ensuring officer safety, efficient problem-solving, and fostering a positive work environment.

Communication is key:

- Clear and concise communication: Develop a clear and concise communication style with your partner. This includes verbal communication during calls, as well as non-verbal cues that signal potential hazards or intentions.

- Active listening: Practice active listening, paying close attention to your partner's updates, observations, and concerns. Acknowledge their input and ensure they feel heard and valued.

- Pre-call briefings: Establish a routine for brief pre-call discussions. Quickly share information about the nature of the call, potential risks, and a plan of action to approach the situation collaboratively.

Collaboration builds a stronger team:

- Shared roles and responsibilities: Clearly define shared roles and responsibilities during patrols. This could involve one officer taking point on traffic stops while the other focuses on crowd control at an event, ensuring a coordinated response.

- Mutual trust and respect: Develop a foundation of mutual trust and respect with your partner. Knowing you can rely on your partner's skills and judgment fosters confidence and a sense of security during patrols.

- Anticipating each other's needs: Over time, you'll develop an understanding of each other's strengths and weaknesses. Learn to anticipate your partner's needs and anticipate situations where they might require backup or support.

Effective communication and collaboration benefit everyone:

- Enhanced officer safety: Clear communication and a shared understanding of situations minimize confusion and allow for coordinated responses, ultimately enhancing officer safety.

- Improved problem-solving: Working together as a team allows you to leverage each other's strengths and perspectives, leading to more effective problem-solving and decision-making during critical incidents.

- Positive work environment: A strong partnership fosters a sense of camaraderie and support, making challenging situations more manageable and fostering a more positive work environment.

By prioritizing clear communication, collaboration, and mutual respect, you and your patrol partner can build a cohesive unit that effectively serves and protects the community.

Recognizing signs of stress and supporting your partner: a pillar of partnership

The demanding nature of police work can take a toll on anyone. As partners, you not only share the workload but also become keenly aware of each other's well-being. Recognizing the signs of stress in your partner and offering support is a crucial aspect of a strong partnership.

Signs of stress to watch for:

- Changes in behaviour: Notice any significant changes in your partner's behaviour, such as increased irritability, withdrawal from social interaction, or difficulty concentrating.

- Physical manifestations: Stress can manifest physically through changes in sleep patterns, appetite, or a higher frequency of headaches or stomachaches.

- Emotional cues: Pay attention to emotional cues like frustration, anger outbursts, or a sense of detachment.

Offering support and building resilience:

- Open communication: Maintain open communication and create a safe space for your partner to express their concerns without judgment. Listen actively and offer empathy.

- Practical support: Look for ways to offer practical support during particularly stressful periods. This could involve covering some workload, helping with paperwork, or simply offering to run errands.

- Encouraging help-seeking: If your partner is struggling to cope, gently encourage them to seek professional help. Offer to accompany them to therapy appointments or help them research resources.

Remember, you're not a therapist, but you can be a source of strength:

• Active listening: Sometimes, all your partner needs is a listening ear and someone to validate their feelings. Active listening demonstrates your support and can be a powerful tool for emotional processing.

• Positive reinforcement: Acknowledge your partner's resilience and coping mechanisms. Positive reinforcement can help them feel more confident in their ability to handle stress.

• Self-care reminder: Gently remind your partner of the importance of self-care. Encourage them to prioritize healthy sleep, exercise, and activities they enjoy to manage stress effectively.

By recognizing the signs of stress and offering support, you become a pillar of strength for your partner. This fosters a strong working relationship built on mutual trust and respect, allowing you to navigate challenges together and ensure each other's well-being throughout your service.

Building trust and mutual respect within the partnership: the foundation of success

The foundation of any successful police partnership is built on a bedrock of trust and mutual respect. These qualities go beyond simple courtesy and create a working environment where officers feel confident, supported, and empowered to perform their duties effectively.

Here's how to cultivate trust and respect within your partnership:

• Open and honest communication: Maintain open and honest communication with your partner. Share your observations, concerns, and even mistakes in a transparent manner. Being upfront fosters trust and allows for collaborative problem-solving.

• Acknowledging strengths and weaknesses: Recognize and appreciate each other's strengths and weaknesses. Understanding these differences will enable you to rely on each other's expertise and compensate for areas where one might need support.

• Respecting boundaries: Respect your partner's boundaries, both professional and personal. This includes respecting their preferred communication styles, work habits, and need for personal space during patrols.

Actions speak louder than words:

- Reliability and dependability: Always strive to be reliable and dependable for your partner. Knowing they can count on you in any situation builds trust and fosters a sense of security.

- Active listening and empathy: Practice active listening and demonstrate empathy towards your partner's experiences and challenges. Show genuine interest in their well-being and offer support when needed.

- Shared decision-making: Whenever possible, involve your partner in decision-making processes. Consider their perspectives and value their input, fostering a sense of shared responsibility and ownership over the work you do together.

The benefits of trust and mutual respect are numerous:

- Enhanced officer safety: Knowing you can trust your partner to have your back in any situation allows for more coordinated responses and ultimately enhances officer safety.

- Improved problem-solving: Working as a team with mutual respect allows you to leverage each other's strengths and perspectives, leading to more effective problem-solving and better outcomes.

- Positive work environment: A partnership built on trust and respect fosters a positive work environment where officers feel comfortable, valued, and motivated to perform their best.

By prioritizing open communication, acknowledging individual strengths, and demonstrating respect, you and your partner can build an unbreakable bond. This foundation of trust and mutual respect will empower you to face any challenge together, ensuring a successful and fulfilling partnership.

Utilizing each other's strengths for optimal results: a team advantage

The success of a police partnership hinges not just on trust and respect but also on capitalizing on each other's strengths. By recognizing and leveraging your partner's unique skills and experiences, you can create a formidable team that delivers optimal results.

Identifying individual strengths:

- Self-awareness: Be introspective about your own strengths and weaknesses. What are you particularly skilled at? In what areas could you benefit from your partner's expertise?

- Open communication: Openly discuss each other's strengths and areas for development. This allows you to assign tasks and approach situations in a way that optimizes your combined skillset.

- Past experiences: Consider your partner's background and past experiences. They might have expertise in de-escalation tactics, crisis intervention, or specific aspects of criminal investigation.

Optimizing performance through collaboration:

- Task delegation: Delegate tasks based on strengths. If your partner excels at building rapport with civilians, they might take point during community interactions while you handle tasks requiring strong analytical skills.

- Complementary skillsets: Recognize how your strengths complement each other. A more assertive partner might lead in high-pressure situations, while a more patient officer can provide a calming influence.

- Continuous learning: Be open to learning from each other. If your partner excels in a particular area, ask them to share their knowledge and expertise. This fosters mutual growth and strengthens your teamwork.

The benefits of leveraging strengths are numerous:

- Enhanced problem-solving: By combining your areas of expertise, you can approach problems from multiple angles, leading to more creative and effective solutions.

- Improved efficiency: Delegation based on strengths allows you to work more efficiently, completing tasks quickly and accurately.

- Increased confidence: Knowing you have a partner who complements your skillset fosters confidence in your abilities to handle any situation that arises.

Remember, a strong partnership is more than the sum of its parts. By recognizing each other's strengths and working together effectively, you can create a team that delivers exceptional results while fostering a sense of accomplishment and shared purpose in your police work.

LEGAL CONSIDERATIONS AND REPORT WRITING

Understanding relevant laws and department policies: a foundation for effective action

Police work is a complex field governed by laws and departmental policies. A thorough understanding of these regulations is crucial for officers to perform their duties effectively and legally.

• Relevant Laws: Officers must have a strong grasp of the laws they enforce, including criminal codes, traffic regulations, and use-of-force guidelines. Understanding the legal framework ensures their actions are justified and fall within the boundaries of their authority.

• Department Policies: In addition to broader laws, each department has its own set of policies that govern officer conduct, procedures, and reporting requirements. Familiarization with these policies ensures officers adhere to departmental standards and maintain consistency in their approach to various situations.

Here's how understanding these regulations benefits officers:

• Reduced legal liability: A strong understanding of relevant laws and policies minimizes the risk of legal action arising from misunderstandings or procedural errors.

• Increased confidence: Knowing the legal boundaries and departmental expectations empowers officers to make informed decisions and act confidently in the field.

• Enhanced professionalism: Adherence to legal and departmental guidelines fosters a sense of professionalism and ensures officers uphold the highest standards of conduct.

Staying up-to-date is critical:

• Regular training: Departments often provide ongoing training to keep officers updated on changes in laws and departmental policies. Actively participating in such training ensures officers stay current with the latest legal developments.

• Seeking clarification: If there's any uncertainty regarding a specific law or policy, don't hesitate to seek clarification from supervisors or legal counsel. It's always better to be certain than to act on incomplete information.

Understanding relevant laws and department policies is not just a professional obligation; it's a cornerstone of effective police work.

By staying informed and adhering to legal and departmental guidelines, officers can ensure their actions are lawful and ethical and contribute to a well-functioning justice system.

Accurate and comprehensive report writing: the power of documentation

Thorough and accurate report writing is a fundamental aspect of police work. These reports serve as a vital record of events, providing a clear and objective account of interactions with the public, investigations conducted, and actions taken. Here's why comprehensive reporting is so crucial:

• Legal Documentation: Police reports are often used as evidence in court proceedings. Accurate and detailed documentation ensures a clear picture of the events for judges, juries, and attorneys.

• Transparency and Accountability: Detailed reports promote transparency and accountability within the justice system. They provide a record of officers' actions and decisions, allowing for oversight and review.

- Investigative Tool: Well-written reports can be invaluable investigative tools. Details documented at the scene can serve as a roadmap for further investigation and can help identify potential leads or witnesses.

Here's what makes a report accurate and comprehensive:

- Factual objectivity: Reports should be based on facts and observations, avoiding personal opinions or emotional biases. Focus on presenting a clear and concise account of what transpired.

- Specificity and Detail: Include specific details like dates, times, locations, descriptions of people and events, and any relevant witness statements. The more details included the more precise the picture of the situation.

- Chronological Order: Organize the report chronologically, outlining the sequence of events from the initial call to the conclusion of the officer's involvement. This ensures a clear understanding of the progression of the situation.

Developing strong report writing skills benefits everyone:

- Enhanced Court Outcomes: Accurate and comprehensive reports can strengthen the prosecution's case and ensure that justice is served.

- Improved Officer Safety: Detailed reports can protect officers from false accusations or misunderstandings by providing a clear record of their actions.

- Effective Communication: Strong writing skills allow officers to communicate effectively with colleagues, supervisors, and the legal system, ensuring everyone involved has a clear understanding of the case.

Remember, accurate and comprehensive report writing is not just a task; it's a professional responsibility. By prioritizing detailed documentation, officers contribute to a more transparent and effective justice system, ensuring their actions are documented accurately and contribute to positive outcomes.

Documenting events and actions in a clear and concise manner: capturing the essence of the encounter

Police reports are the backbone of effective communication within the legal system. However, crafting clear and concise narratives is essential for ensuring critical details are preserved in a sea of information. Here's how officers can document events and actions effectively:

- Focus on Objectivity: Strive for factual accuracy and avoid embellishment or emotional language. Present a neutral and unbiased account of the situation, focusing on what you saw, heard, and did.

- Prioritize Clarity: Use clear and concise language that is easy to understand. Avoid technical jargon or legal terminology that might be confusing to a broader audience.

- Organize for Readability: Structure your report logically, with a clear beginning, middle, and end. Utilize bullet points or numbered lists when outlining sequences of events or witness statements.

Capturing key details is paramount:

- The 5 Ws and 1 H: Employ the journalistic approach by answering the who, what, when, where, why, and how of the situation. This ensures all essential elements of the encounter are documented.

- Accurate Descriptions: Provide detailed descriptions of people involved, locations, and any relevant objects encountered. Focus on specific details like clothing, distinguishing features, or unique characteristics that aid in the identification or reconstruction of events.

- Timeline Construction: Establish a clear timeline of events, outlining the sequence of actions from the initial call for service through the conclusion of your involvement.

Conciseness doesn't equate to omitting crucial details:

- Selective Detail: While comprehensiveness is important, avoid including irrelevant information that might cloud the central narrative. Focus on details that directly contribute to understanding the situation and the officer's actions.

- Summarize when appropriate: If lengthy conversations occur, summarize the key points and main takeaways instead of including a verbatim transcript.

Clear and concise documentation benefits everyone:

- Enhanced Court Efficiency: Streamlined reports save court time by ensuring judges and juries can readily grasp the situation and focus on crucial details.

- Improved Communication: Clear reports facilitate better communication between officers, detectives, and legal teams, ensuring everyone involved has a

 consistent understanding of the case.

- Reduced Misconceptions: Accurate and concise documentation minimizes the risk of misunderstandings or misinterpretations, ensuring a clearer picture of events for all parties involved.

By prioritizing clarity, conciseness, and capturing essential details, officers can craft reports that effectively communicate the essence of an encounter. These well-documented narratives contribute to a more efficient legal system and ensure officers' actions are accurately represented.

Courtroom testimony and evidence presentation: delivering a compelling account

Police officers are frequently called upon to present evidence and testify in court. Their ability to provide a clear, confident, and professional presentation can significantly impact the outcome of a case. Here's how officers can excel in the courtroom:

• Reviewing Case Details: Before appearing in court, thoroughly review the case file, police reports, and any collected evidence. This ensures you have a clear understanding of questions accurately.

• Anticipating Questions: Practice anticipating potential questions from both the prosecution and the defence.

Rehearse clear and concise answers that focus on factual details documented in your reports.

• Maintaining Composure: Courtroom environments can be stressful. However, remaining calm, composed, and respectful throughout your testimony projects professionalism and strengthens the credibility of your account.

Effective evidence presentation is key:

• Understanding Chain of Custody: Be prepared to explain the chain of custody for any evidence you present. This demonstrates that evidence has been handled appropriately and hasn't been tampered with.

• Clarity and Conciseness: When presenting evidence, focus on clear and concise explanations. Avoid technical jargon or overly complex language. Tailor your explanations to the judge or jury's level of understanding.

• Professional Demeanor: Maintain a professional demeanor throughout your presentation. Avoid using slang, emotional language, or personal opinions. Focus on presenting the facts in a neutral and objective manner.

Confidence inspires trust:

• Speak Clearly and Confidently: Project your voice and speak clearly. Avoid mumbling or rushing through your testimony. Confidence in your recollection of events fosters trust in your account.

• Truthfulness and Accuracy: Remember, your primary obligation is to the truth. Be honest and forthcoming in your answers, even if they seem unfavourable to the prosecution's case.

Delivering a compelling courtroom presentation goes beyond simply recounting events. By preparing meticulously, maintaining composure, and presenting evidence clearly, officers can significantly contribute to the legal process and ensure their accounts are presented accurately and effectively.

CONTINUING EDUCATION AND PROFESSIONAL DEVELOPMENT

Importance of ongoing training and skill development: a commitment to excellence

The field of law enforcement is constantly evolving, with new techniques, technologies, and legal precedents emerging all the time.

To remain effective and adaptable, officers must commit to ongoing training and professional development.

Here's why continuous learning is essential:

• Enhancing Skills and Knowledge: Ongoing training equips officers with the latest knowledge, skills, and procedures. This could involve training in de-escalation tactics, crisis intervention techniques, advancements in forensic science, or updates on use-of-force guidelines.

• Staying Informed of Legal Developments: Laws and legal interpretations can change over time. Regular training ensures officers stay current on these developments, allowing them to perform their duties within the legal framework and adapt their approach accordingly.

• Building Expertise: Specialized training allows officers to develop expertise in specific areas like traffic enforcement, K-9 handling, or criminal investigations. This diversification of skills strengthens the overall capacity of the department.

The benefits of continuous learning extend beyond technical expertise:

• Improved Officer Safety: Training in new tactics and technologies equips officers with the tools to handle dangerous situations more effectively, ultimately enhancing their safety on the job.

• Increased Confidence: A solid knowledge base and mastery of relevant skills fosters confidence in officers' abilities to navigate complex situations and make sound decisions.

• Building Stronger Relationships: Exposure to diverse perspectives and best practices through training programs can foster collaboration and understanding between officers from different departments or backgrounds.

Investing in ongoing training is an investment in public safety. By continuously developing their skills and knowledge, officers remain at the forefront of effective law enforcement, able to adapt to evolving challenges and serve their communities with the highest level of competence and professionalism.

Staying up-to-date on new laws, procedures, and technologies: navigating a dynamic landscape

The landscape of law enforcement is constantly shifting. New legislation, evolving procedures, and emerging technologies necessitate a commitment from officers to stay abreast of these changes. Here's why staying current is crucial for effective police work:

• Maintaining Legal Compliance: Police actions must adhere to the law. Regular updates on legal developments, particularly regarding use-of-force guidelines, search and seizure protocols, and evolving case law, ensure officers operate within the legal framework and protect themselves from potential liability.

• Optimizing Procedures: Departmental procedures are constantly reviewed and refined to enhance efficiency and effectiveness. Staying informed of these updates allows officers to adapt their approach and leverage the latest best practices to improve outcomes in various situations.

• Embracing Technological Advancements: Technology plays an increasingly central role in law enforcement. Familiarization with new tools, from crime scene investigation equipment to data analysis software, empowers officers to gather evidence more effectively, improve communication, and enhance overall efficiency.

Staying informed requires a proactive approach:

• Departmental Training: Departments often provide ongoing training to keep officers updated on legal changes, procedural updates, and emerging technologies. Actively participating in such programs ensures officers stay current with the latest developments.

• Professional Associations: Professional law enforcement associations offer resources and training opportunities to keep members informed on new trends and best practices. Membership fosters a sense of community and allows officers to learn from colleagues across jurisdictions.

• Industry Publications: Staying informed through industry publications, online resources, and legal journals allows officers to take ownership of their professional development and stay ahead of the curve.

The benefits of staying current are numerous:

- Enhanced Public Trust: Officers who demonstrate a commitment to legal compliance, best practices, and technological advancements project a sense of professionalism and foster public trust in law enforcement.

- Improved Problem-Solving: Understanding new technologies and procedures allows officers to approach problems from multiple angles, leading to more creative and effective solutions in the field.

- Safer Work Environment: Familiarity with updated tactics and technologies equips officers to navigate potentially dangerous situations more effectively, ultimately enhancing safety for themselves and the public.

By actively seeking out opportunities to learn and stay informed, officers demonstrate a dedication to excellence in their profession.

This commitment ensures they can face any challenge with confidence and knowledge, ultimately contributing to a safer and more just community.

Seeking mentorship and peer support opportunities: building a network for growth

The path of a police officer is rarely a solitary one.

Seasoned veterans can offer invaluable guidance while connecting with colleagues can provide support and a sense of shared purpose. Here's how mentorship and peer support opportunities can benefit officers:

• Mentorship: Pairing with experienced officers provides access to a wealth of knowledge and practical experience. Mentors can offer guidance on navigating complex situations, developing professional skills, and coping with the emotional challenges of the job.

• Peer Support: Connecting with colleagues who understand the daily realities of police work fosters a sense of camaraderie and belonging. Peer support networks provide safe spaces to share experiences, vent frustrations, and encourage one another.

Mentorship provides invaluable guidance:

• Learning from Experience: Experienced officers can share insights and strategies they've developed. This practical knowledge can help new officers navigate similar situations more confidently and effectively.

• Building Confidence: A supportive mentor can boost confidence, particularly when facing new challenges or difficult decisions. Mentors can provide reassurance and offer alternative perspectives to consider.

• Developing Professional Skills: Mentors can guide officers in honing specific skills, such as communication techniques, conflict resolution, and report writing. Their feedback can be invaluable in fostering professional development.

Peer support fosters a sense of community:

• Shared Understanding: Peers who face similar challenges on the job can offer a sense of shared understanding and belonging. They can empathize with the emotional toll of police work and provide a safe space for open communication.

• Stress Management: Peer support networks can be a source of coping mechanisms and stress management strategies. Sharing experiences and offering encouragement can help officers manage the emotional burden of the job.

• Strengthening Resilience: Knowing they have a network of colleagues for support fosters resilience in officers. Peer support can help them bounce back from challenging situations and maintain a sense of well-being throughout their careers.

Officers invest in professional growth and personal well-being by seeking mentors and participating in peer support networks.

These connections offer guidance, support, and a sense of community, empowering officers to confidently and resiliently navigate the complexities of police work.

Maintaining professional integrity and ethical conduct: the cornerstone of trust

Upholding the highest standards of professional integrity and ethical conduct is the cornerstone of effective law enforcement.

Police officers serve as representatives of the law, and their actions directly impact public trust in the justice system. Here's how officers can consistently demonstrate ethical behaviour:

- Adherence to the Law and Policies: Officers have a fundamental responsibility for upholding policies. This includes avoiding shortcuts, following proper procedures, and using their authority ethically and within legal boundaries.

- Transparency and Accountability: Honesty and transparency are paramount. Officers should be truthful in their reports, interactions with the public, and court testimony. They should also be accountable for their actions and decisions.

- Respect for All: Treat everyone with dignity and respect, regardless of background, ethnicity, or socioeconomic status. Building positive relationships with the community fosters trust and cooperation.

Ethical conduct goes beyond legal compliance:

- Avoiding Conflicts of Interest: Officers should be mindful of potential conflicts of interest and avoid situations where personal gain could influence their professional judgment.

- Whistle-Blowing: If officers witness unethical conduct by colleagues, they are responsible for reporting it through proper channels. Speaking up against wrongdoing protects the integrity of the profession.

- Maintaining Emotional Control: Police work can be emotionally demanding. However, maintaining composure and avoiding actions fueled by anger, bias, or prejudice is crucial for upholding ethical conduct.

The benefits of ethical conduct are far-reaching:

- Public Trust: When officers demonstrate ethical behaviour, they foster public trust in law enforcement. This cooperation between police and the community is essential for effective crime prevention and maintaining a safe environment.

- Professional Satisfaction: Adhering to high ethical standards allows officers to take pride in their work and maintain a sense of professionalism.

- Stronger Justice System: Ethical conduct within law enforcement strengthens the entire justice system by ensuring fairness and upholding the rule of law.

Maintaining professional integrity and ethical conduct is not a one-time act; it's a continuous commitment. By consistently making ethical choices, officers can ensure their actions reflect the values they represent and contribute to a more just and secure community.

CONCLUSIONS

The path of a police officer is demanding and requires a unique blend of skills and attributes. While physical fitness and tactical proficiency are essential, psychological resilience, effective teamwork, and a commitment to professional development are equally crucial for success in this complex profession.

The Psychological Landscape of Policing

The psychological demands of police work are significant. Officers routinely face stressful and unpredictable situations, requiring them to make critical decisions under pressure. Developing emotional intelligence allows officers to manage stress effectively, maintain composure in high-pressure scenarios, and foster empathy in their interactions with the public. Furthermore, cultivating mental well-being through healthy coping mechanisms is essential for long-term resilience and career satisfaction.

The Power of Teamwork

Effective law enforcement is rarely a solitary endeavour.

Police officers rely on strong partnerships with their colleagues to navigate challenging situations and achieve optimal results. Building trust and respect within teams fosters open communication and allows officers to leverage each other's strengths. Recognizing and appreciating individual skill sets empowers team members to collaborate effectively and approach problems from multiple angles.

Strong teamwork ensures a more comprehensive response to complex situations, enhancing officer safety and public well-being.

The Importance of Legal Considerations and Report Writing

Police work hinges on a solid understanding of the law and departmental policies. Adherence to legal boundaries protects officers from liability and justifies their actions. Furthermore, thorough and accurate report writing is the backbone of effective communication within the justice system. Detailed reports provide a clear picture of events for judges, juries, and investigators, fostering transparency and accountability within the legal process.

By prioritizing clear and concise documentation, officers ensure their actions are accurately represented and contribute to favourable legal outcomes.

Continuing Education and Professional Development

The field of law enforcement is constantly evolving. New laws are enacted, procedures are refined, and technologies emerge rapidly. Officers who commit to ongoing training and professional development remain at the forefront of effective policing. This commitment allows them to adapt to new challenges, enhance their skill sets, and stay informed on legal developments and best practices.

Ultimately, ongoing learning strengthens the overall capacity of the department and contributes to a safer and more just community.

Maintaining Professional Integrity and Ethical Conduct

Upholding the highest standards of professional integrity and ethical conduct is the cornerstone of effective law enforcement.

Police officers serve as representatives of the law, and their actions directly impact public trust in the justice system. Officers build positive relationships with the community and foster cooperation by adhering to the law, acting with transparency and accountability, and treating everyone with respect. Ethical conduct extends beyond legal compliance; actively avoiding conflicts of interest, whistle-blowing when necessary, and maintaining emotional control are all essential for upholding the profession's integrity. Officers who consistently make ethical choices demonstrate a commitment to justice and contribute to a more robust, trustworthy legal system.

The Road to Success

Becoming a well-rounded officer is a journey, not a destination. It requires dedication to physical fitness, ongoing psychological development, fostering strong partnerships, and ethical conduct and professional learning. By embracing these various aspects of police work, officers can navigate the profession's complexities with confidence, resilience, and an unwavering commitment to serving their communities.

The path of a police officer is paved with challenges and rewards in equal measure. It's a profession that demands courage, compassion, and an unwavering dedication to justice. As you embark on this journey, let the words of Helen Keller serve as a guiding light:

"Your true success is measured by the strength of your desire, the height of your dreams, and the depth of your commitment."

Thank you very much for buying this book and reading it to the end.

Now, we would like to ask you a small favour. Please take a minute or two to leave a review for this book on Amazon. This feedback will significantly help us; please let us know if you like the book.

Thanks again!

ABOUT THE AUTHOR

Dott. Gianmarco Scaglioso, local police officer and founder of *www.concorsipoliziamunicipale.it* is a training portal for recruiting local police personnel.

www.ingramcontent.com/pod-product-compliance
Lightning Source LLC
Chambersburg PA
CBHW052300220526
45471CB00001B/417